Seeing the
Unseen

The Mystery of God's Hidden
Hand in the Book of Esther

Christopher Culver

ISBN 978-1-64492-617-8 (paperback)
ISBN 978-1-64492-618-5 (digital)

Christian Faith Publishing, Inc.
832 Park Avenue
Meadville, PA 16335
www.christianfaithpublishing.com

Printed in the United States of America

To my wife, Denise, who has walked life's rocky and often puzzling path with me. Your unfaltering devotion to our Lord, even in the darkest nights, has helped me learn what it is to endure in faith as seeing him who is unseen.

For our light and momentary affliction produces for us an eternal weight of glory, far beyond all comparison. And so we fix our gaze, not on the things which are seen, but the things which are unseen, for the things which are seen are passing, but the things which are unseen are eternal.
—2 Corinthians 4:17–18

Contents

Introduction

"Who knows whether you have not attained royalty for such a time as this?" These words, spoken to Esther by her cousin, Mordecai, pointed to the astonishing turn of events that had seen a young Jewish woman emerge from complete obscurity to become the queen of the mightiest empire the world had ever known. Esther hadn't sought this privileged position, and no one among her people could have imagined what was in store for her. For Esther was a *Jew*—an Israelite woman who lived among the Jewish exiles scattered throughout the vast Medo-Persian Empire. She was not a person of nobility or status; quite the opposite, she was part of a small, despised, and powerless minority group. Even more, Esther was a young *female* Jew in a world defined by male authority and power and Persian culture. How could such a person find herself the beloved wife and powerful queen of the splendid King Ahasuerus, sovereign ruler of the Medes and Persians, the man whose dominion stretched from India to Africa? One could hardly imagine a less likely circumstance, and this caused Esther's cousin to wonder whether divine power and purpose lay behind it. He knew that death and destruction loomed on the horizon for the Jewish people; perhaps this was why Esther found herself enthroned as queen; perhaps she had indeed attained royalty for just such a time as this.

This is the story the book of Esther tells. It is a marvelous story, but one easily passed over in the Old Testament scriptures. Set alongside such majestic writings as the prophets Isaiah, Jeremiah, Ezekiel, and Daniel, the little book of Esther can seem to pale in significance. It doesn't contain lofty doctrine or mysterious prophecies; in fact, the story doesn't even mention God. It simply follows the experiences of two Jewish cousins, Esther and Mordecai, who lived during the time of Israel's exile following the Babylonian conquest of Jerusalem in 586 BC.

And so, one might ask the question: Why Esther? Why should a person care about this little book? For one thing, Esther was a gracious, courageous, and faithful woman, and many Christians have been encouraged and strengthened in their faith by her story. But does the book of Esther play a larger role in the Bible, and if so, what is that role? The answer begins with recognizing that the Esther story is an important part of the larger story that begins with God's work of creation and reaches its climax in the person of Jesus of Nazareth. The Old Testament tells the story of God's purposes for the world and how he was going to achieve them. It reveals that God was going to accomplish his designs through a certain person who'd emerge among the people of Israel at the appointed time. Jesus was that person, and this is why he could say that the Old Testament writings speak of him (Luke 24:25–27, 44–45; John 5:39).

The book of Esther, then, matters because it plays a crucial role in the larger Old Testament story whose grand subject is Jesus the Messiah. But how can a book that doesn't even mention God have anything to do with God's incarnate Son? Was Jesus including the book of Esther when he insisted that all of the Scriptures are about him? And if so, how is that the case? These questions show how important it is to read and interpret Esther correctly—to understand it the way the Bible understands it. It is more than an ancient Jewish story about a certain period in Israel's long history. It sketches a beautiful and engaging portrait of a remarkable young woman, but it does far more; the book of Esther adds its critical voice to the Scripture's witness to Jesus Christ and God's glorious work in him.

Allowed to tell its own story, the book of Esther is a captivating tale of danger, intrigue, conspiracy, and courage carried along by a winding river of twists and turns. Every time the reader thinks he knows what to expect, he comes face-to-face with the unexpected. In a way that is both mysterious and thrilling, the Esther story reveals an ever-faithful God who accomplishes his unchanging will for the world, not in the whirlwind but the still, small voice; not with spectacular displays of power, but with an unremarkable, and often undetected, hand. The book of Esther exalts the unseen, seemingly silent God whose loving designs are unchanging and undaunted, the God who, in every circumstance, is worthy of our complete trust and devotion.

May the sovereign Lord and loving Father who is the unsung hero of the Esther story be pleased to use this present treatment to grant the reader a fresh and deeper gaze into his glory that is in the face of Christ.

Chapter 1
Background

The Esther story is an ancient one. Its setting and circumstances and the manner of life it describes are very distant and foreign to modern readers and the world they know. But this story has enjoyed a prominent place in the history and religious life of the Jewish people up to the present day. So much so that it is the focal point of one of the great celebrations in the Jewish calendar, namely the festival of Purim.[1]

The Jews afford this status to the Esther story because they recognize its vital contribution to the larger story of Israel; it adds its voice to the written record that chronicles their history as the covenant children of Abraham, Isaac, and Jacob. The Esther story is important to the Jewish people and their religious life, but it ought to be just as important to those who aren't Jews. It is a Jewish story, but its main character is the One who is the God of all people; the God who created the world and whose hand continues to lovingly direct his world toward the marvelous goal he's ordained for it. In this story, we see the heart and hand of the unseen God—often undetected, but always working powerfully and effectively—and this should capture the attention and imagination of all people everywhere.

The book of Esther concerns events involving the Israelite people which occurred in the fifth century BC during the time of their exile from the land of Canaan. As with much of the Old Testament,

---

[1] The book of Esther is one of the *Megilloth* (rolls)—the five books of the Hebrew Bible associated with five particular holidays. The *Megilloth* consists of *Ruth* (Pentecost), *Song of Solomon* (Passover), *Ecclesiastes* (the Feast of Booths), *Lamentations* (Ninth of Ab), and *Esther* (Purim).

the author of Esther is unknown, so that information about the book's origin must come from the account itself and other historical data. The story's epilogue indicates that the account was written subsequent to the reign of the Persian king Ahasuerus (Xerxes), which ended in 464 BC (Est. 10:1–2). So, the author's familiarity with Persian customs and details associated with Ahasuerus's reign suggests that he lived in Persia during the general time period addressed in the book. This conclusion is reinforced by the writer's intimate knowledge of the events, circumstances, and interactions he recounted. The festival of Purim provides another dating clue. The book of Esther addresses the institution of this festival and the earliest known historical reference to Purim dates to the Maccabean period of Israel's history (second century BC). This strongly suggests that Esther was written by that time.

The Jewish Talmud teaches that Mordecai (one of the book's main characters) wrote the original text, but this is a matter of tradition, not clear evidence. At the same time, the book's Jewish perspective and orientation make it virtually certain that the author was a Jew. Given the Jews' status in the Gentile world of that time, one can hardly imagine a non-Jew composing such an account. In the end, most conservative scholars hold that the original manuscript was written by a Jew by the beginning of the fourth century BC, after the death of the Persian king Ahasuerus, but before the time of Alexander the Great.

The book of Esther has many interesting and unique features, but perhaps the most notable is the obvious absence of any mention of God. This sets it apart from every other writing in the Hebrew and Christian scriptures. While the story has Israel's covenant relationship with God as its sub-text, the text itself simply recounts the historical episode behind the Jewish festival of Purim. The book is also fiercely nationalistic in its Jewishness, and these considerations (among others) have caused Esther's place in the Christian Bible to be debated and even contested in Church history. Martin Luther's comment is illustrative, "I am so hostile to this book (II Maccabees) and to Esther that I would wish they did not exist at all; for they Judaize too greatly and have much heathenish impropriety."

Historical Context

The Esther story is set in the period of the Jewish exile following Judah's conquest by the Babylonians, who were the dominant Middle Eastern power at that time. The Babylonian king, Nebuchadnezzar, established his control over Judah in 605 BC and enthroned Zedekiah as his vassal lord in Jerusalem some eight years later. But after nine years on the throne, Zedekiah revolted against Babylonian authority, leading Nebuchadnezzar to return to Judah and lay siege to Jerusalem. His strategy was to surround and isolate the city and then wait for famine and disease to do their work. Two years later, in 586 BC, with Jerusalem's residents sick and starving, Nebuchadnezzar breached the city walls, tore the temple to the ground, burned the city, and took the survivors in chains to Babylon (2 Kings 24:17–25:21; 2 Chron. 36:10–21; cf. also Jer. 52:1–30).

Babylonian rule over Judah continued for the next five decades until Cyrus, the young ruler of Medo-Persia, seized control of the Babylonian kingdom in 539 BC in a whirlwind conquest. In an ingenious move, he conquered the fortified city of Babylon by diverting the Euphrates River, which flowed into the city underneath the city wall. Cyrus then used the dry riverbed to move his army into the city while the people were preoccupied in a time of feasting.

Shortly after his conquest of the Babylonian kingdom, and in fulfillment of God's word through his prophet Isaiah (Isa. 44:28), Cyrus issued a decree in 538 BC allowing the Jewish exiles to return to Jerusalem and rebuild the temple and the city (2 Chron. 36:22–23; Ezra 1:1–4). Many Jews returned to Judah (Ezra 2:1–65), but many others chose to remain in the cities and villages outside the land of Israel where the Babylonians had relocated them. Some eighty years later (457 BC), another company of exiles would return to Jerusalem under Ezra's leadership (Ezra 7), followed about twelve years later by a third group led by Nehemiah (Neh. 1–2).

Esther lived during the period between the first and second return episodes (Ezra 4:6) and, like so many exiled Jews, her family had decided to remain behind rather than make the journey back to Judea. Residing in Susa, the capital of the Medo-Persian Empire

(Est. 2:5–7; cf. also Neh. 1:1–3), Esther and her cousin, Mordecai, exemplified the people of Israel in their exile and dispersion among the nations.

Redemptive Historical Context

The "redemptive-historical" context refers to the setting of a particular biblical text within the movement and development of God's work of redemption. The Old Testament scriptures recount historical circumstances and events extending from the creation of the world to shortly before the birth of Jesus Christ. But the Old Testament isn't concerned with world history as such, but the *history of redemption*—that is, the purposeful and orderly history of God's activity in the world toward his goal of redeeming and restoring his creation in his Son, Jesus the Messiah.

This orientation and purpose are often overlooked in reading and interpreting the Old Testament scriptures, but are critically important. Some approach the Bible as if every book (if not every individual passage) stands on its own, but this is not the case. The fact that the Bible is a *historical* account shows that each book and context is related to all others by its place within the flow of history. So, for instance, one must read Isaiah's prophecy in view of when it occurred in history and what came before it. So, the four gospel accounts presume all of the Old Testament history as their backdrop.

All of the content in the Bible is related historically, but history itself has a structure, flow, and goal. This truth lies behind the concept of "redemptive history." History isn't an endless chain of independent circumstances and events, but a divinely-orchestrated scheme. History is *his story*—God's work in the world to bring his creation to its final destiny. And this destiny involves the creation's redemption, which is to say, its deliverance from the curse that came upon it at the fall of man. Biblical history, then, is the history of redemption, and this means that it isn't sufficient to identify the historical context of a biblical writing. *Knowing the "who, what, where and when" of a scriptural text is critically important, but it's even more important to understand where that text fits within the unfolding history of God's work of redemption.* A driver needs to be aware of his location as he makes his way down a road, but the *meaning* of his location is determined by the journey he's on. The meaning of the parts is in the whole.

The Old Testament scriptures trace out God's activity in the world directed toward what he promised in Eden, namely a son of Eve appointed to conquer the serpent, destroy his works, and bring life out of death to the cursed creation (Gen. 3:14–24, esp. vv. 15, 20). And by chronicling God's work toward that ordained goal, the Scriptures provide insight into God's person and mind. But this revelation unfolds progressively as history itself progresses. God's revelation in the Scriptures develops like brushstrokes in a painting—each stroke of the artist's brush looks back to and builds on those he's already set to the canvas. But that process has a goal in mind; it works toward the final painting that already exists in the artist's mind. Each brushstroke finds its meaning in its contribution to the finished work, but that contribution depends on it being properly related to all other brushstrokes. This is how it is with the Scripture and the way it reveals truth: each stage of revelation—situated within a historical context—looks back to and builds on what came before, but with an eye to what is yet to come. Scriptural revelation is *progressive* and *organic* (fitted together in a unified whole), so that the meaning of any biblical text derives from its place within and contribution to the "big picture" of God's revealed design.

And because God's design for the world is bound up in Jesus Christ, every biblical text has a fundamental *Christ-centeredness*. This doesn't imply or suggest that every passage in the Old Testament directly concerns or speaks about Jesus; rather, the Old Testament scriptures are "Christ-centered" in the sense that Jesus the Messiah (the *Christ*) is the focal point in God's plan for his creation and that plan is revealed, developed, interpreted, and worked out in the scriptural writings. The Old Testament scriptures trace God's actions and interactions as he prepared for the coming and redemptive work of his incarnate Son; this means that the Old Testament in its entirety must be understood as the revelation of Jesus Christ. This is exactly the sense in which Jesus—and his disciples after him—affirmed that all of the Scriptures (meaning the Old Testament writings) testify of him (cf. Luke 24:25–27, 44–45; Acts 3:18, 13:14–41, 26:22–23).

And so, just as every scriptural passage has a historical context, it also has a *redemptive-historical* context; it is set at a certain point in the unfolding history of God's work of redemption. With respect to the redemptive-historical context of the book of Esther, one must begin in Genesis 3:15 with God's promise of a triumphal "seed" (offspring). The reason is that this promise set out in germinal form God's intent for the world as it had come under the curse of sin and death. This is why Genesis 3:15 is often referred to as the *protoevangelium*, or "first gospel."

Again, the heart of the protoevangelium was God's promise to Eve of a male offspring who'd conquer the serpent and bring life out of death, thereby ending the curse. He then gave that promise substantial development when he made a covenant with Abraham to establish a *kingdom* through him. Specifically, God promised to make Abraham's offspring into a great and regal nation and give them control over all the region from the Euphrates River in Mesopotamia to the Nile River in Egypt (Gen. 12:1–3, 15:18). But he also told Abraham that this would not occur until his descendants had spent a long season as slaves under cruel oppression (Gen. 15:13–14).

This slavery came about after Jacob (Abraham's grandson) and his household went to live in Egypt during a time of great famine. But after the ordained four hundred years had elapsed, God raised up Moses to liberate Abraham's family (the twelve tribes of Israel) and bring them into formal covenant union with himself at Sinai. Then he led them through a period of wandering and subsequent conquest under Joshua until the land of Canaan was brought under Israelite rule. By the time of his death, Joshua was able to declare to Israel that all of God's word of promise to Abraham had been fulfilled (Josh. 23:14, cf. 21:43–45).

The following centuries were marked by an overall trend of deepening apostasy within Israel— "every man did what was right in his own eyes" (Judg. 17:6, 21:25). Predictably, this resulted in escalating conflict, moral decline, and division among the twelve tribes.

This tragic era of disunity and decline (a large portion of which is recounted in the book of Judges) continued in Israel until David ascended the throne of Israel as a "man after God's own heart" (1 Sam. 13:1–14, 16:1–13).

David reunited the twelve tribes of Israel and established the dominion, power, and greatness of the Israelite kingdom that God had promised to Abraham. But for all its glory, David's reign was marred by unfaithfulness, which brought disgrace on God's name and his covenant kingdom. The Lord responded with a severe judgment: David's "house"—consisting of his immediate household, his royal dynasty and his kingdom—was going to be torn apart from within by enmity and conflict (2 Sam. 11:1–12:14). This internal strife climaxed during the reign of David's grandson, Rehoboam, resulting in the Israelite kingdom being split into the two sub-kingdoms of Judah and Israel.

From that point forward, the two kingdoms moved steadily toward destruction, exile and captivity. God's prophets continued to warn that the day of his patience and pleading was coming to an end, but, by and large, the people of both Israel and Judah turned a deaf ear. Though their covenant Father had shown himself faithful, merciful, and patient, the two houses of Israel insisted on pursuing the path leading to judgment and destruction. Finally, the northern kingdom of Israel fell to the Assyrians in 722 BC and Judah followed shortly after, with Jerusalem being sacked in 586 BC by the armies of Babylon.

God expelled Abraham's covenant descendants from the land he gave them and scattered them among the nations because they refused to honor his covenant with them. He'd warned their fathers of this before they even entered the land, and now his warning had come to pass (Deut. 29–31). Exiled, powerless, and persecuted for more than a century, many of the Jews had all but lost sight of their God's promise to Eve (Gen. 3:15), the patriarchs (Abraham, Isaac, and Jacob) (Gen. 12:1–3, 26:1–4, 28:10–14), and their beloved King David (2 Sam. 7:1–17). And now an ominous storm cloud was forming on the horizon that threatened to wash away all hope for the future. This was the setting of the Esther story.

Literary Context

The book of Esther is composed as historical narrative, but it also has the qualities of a dramatic epic tale in that it recounts the triumphal deeds of its hero and heroine, Mordecai and Esther. But though the story focuses on Esther and Mordecai, the true hero and central figure is the unnamed, invisible God. The Esther story is a narrative illustration of the operation of divine providence. *Providence* refers to God's active guidance of the affairs and course of the world he created, and Esther and Mordecai highlight the role of human instruments in that work.

Divine providence plays a central role in the book of Esther and thus the story unfolds on two levels: the *natural* level of human intent, action, and expectation, and the *supernatural* level of divine oversight and outcome. The genius of the writer lies in the way he has the supernatural operating entirely beneath the story itself, unmentioned and invisible, never intruding upon, violating, eclipsing, or depreciating the natural. The Esther story is an account of human designs and actions, but ones ultimately yielding a stream of outcomes neither foreseen nor predictable, outcomes driven by an imperceptible power and a transcendent purpose.

The writer has his story unfolding on these two levels, and he continually plays the one against the other. The movement of the surface-level human story leads the reader to expect certain outcomes, but again and again the unexpected occurs, resulting in outcomes which highlight the underlying story of God's designs and faithfulness to them. Thus, a pronounced *irony* permeates the Esther story. In literary terms, irony is a device in which words and expressions are used to convey a meaning which contrasts or contradicts their literal or natural sense. It can take several forms, the most basic of which is an utterance where there is a deliberate contrast between the apparent and intended meanings. This is the irony when a person responds to his stalled car with the words, "Isn't that just great!" *Literary* irony can also be nonverbal, involving the features of plot, setting, characterization, etc. where the writer intends a rhetorical, humorous, or other effect. Events themselves can be ironic when they, their outcomes or effects contradict what is naturally expected. This is the most common use of irony in the book of Esther, and it is especially suitable to the author's goal in telling his story, which is to spotlight God's ever-faithful, though often undetected, hand as he directs all things toward his good purpose for the world he loves.

The Esther story uses irony to highlight God's unseen hand, but with the intent of encouraging and strengthening the faith and patience of God's covenant people, the exiled children of Israel. The book was composed during a period of great difficulty and discouragement for the Jewish people. David's once glorious kingdom was in ruins, and Abraham's "great nation" was now nothing more than a sneering byword among the Gentiles (Lamen. 1–2). Moreover, this once mighty people were scattered outside of their homeland, subjugated to an oppressive Gentile power and seemingly without recourse or hope. And if desolation, exile, and oppression were not enough, the Israelite people were now facing their greatest threat since the Lord delivered them from Egypt and made his covenant with them at Sinai. It is in the context of this perilous circumstance that the writer crafts his tale of deliverance, vindication and triumph.

The book is fiercely nationalistic, but because of the writer's intent that it would remind and encourage his Jewish countrymen that their God remained committed to his covenant promises. In spite of all that had transpired and all that they were experiencing, his oath to Abraham, Isaac, and Jacob stood fast. Esther is a story of faithfulness and triumph—God's faithfulness and triumph, and so the triumph of his covenant people. This is the biblical basis for the jubilant festival of Purim that, to this day, is an important part of the Jewish religious calendar.

But the book of Esther also makes an important contribution to the Scripture's revelation of God's larger purpose of redemption; it, too, is a part of the Scriptures that Jesus insisted testify of him. Its first role was to strengthen the hope and confidence of its original Israelite audience, and thus the Jews still hold it in high regard. But for this very reason, it ministers gospel truth to *Christians*, for God's faithfulness to Abraham's descendants finds its ultimate object in all those, Jew and Gentile, who are Abraham's offspring because of their share in *Jesus*, Abraham's unique "seed" and focal point of God's promise (cf. Gen. 12:1–3 with Gal. 3:15–29; also Eph. 2:11–22).

*****

Why Esther, then? First, because the story plays a crucial role in the history of Israel. And not just Israel in its own right, but Israel as the Abrahamic people chosen by God to be his instrument for fulfilling the promise he made in Eden: Israel, the "seed of Abraham," was to be the conduit for God's blessing going out to all people, even as Israel would give birth to Eve's triumphant "seed" appointed to crush the serpent and his "seed." This victory would see the creation's deliverance from the curse of death inflicted upon it through the serpent's deception. Eve's promised offspring would bring life out of death, and so Adam named her *Eve*, "the mother of all the living" (Gen. 3:1–19).

The book of Esther tells the astonishing story of Jewish deliverance and preservation as the work of the unseen, ever-faithful God upholding his intentions for the world. Come what may, Abraham's descendants—the Israelite people—would continue on because the sovereign Lord could never forsake nor fall short of his promise. Israel would endure from generation to generation until the coming of the particular descendant who was the true object of God's promise to Abraham, the One through whom God's blessing would flow out to all the earth's families.

It's clear why the Esther story is precious to the Jewish people, but it should be just as precious to Christians. For all those who belong to Christ, Jew and Gentile alike, are the ultimate beneficiaries of the covenant faithfulness of Israel's God. The One who kept covenant with Abraham has grafted believers in Jesus, Israel's Messiah, into Abraham's covenant household and made them heirs of the promises given to him (Gal. 3:1–29; Eph. 2:11–3:7). The book of Esther exalts God's unwavering faithfulness to Israel manifested in his delivering and preserving hand; Christians, whether Jewish or Gentile, enjoy the ultimate end to which that faithfulness looked, namely God's great and everlasting deliverance in his Son. Like the

Jews of Esther's day, Christians have been delivered from death and destruction, but in the superlative sense. How much more, then, should believers in Jesus the Messiah exult in the faithful God of Abraham whom the Jewish people celebrate every year at Purim?

So also we, who are Christians, ought to derive from the Esther story the same encouragement and sure hope the writer intended for his Jewish readers. Like Esther and Mordecai, we, too, find that life confronts us with unexpected and threatening circumstances; we, too, often sense that the lot has been cast against us so that all hope is lost. So also our troubles tend to lock our gaze on our experiences and expectations rather than on the purposes and promises of the unseen, unnoticed God. Troubles turn our hearts and minds earthward, but the Esther story reminds us that our troubles are in the hand of the ever-faithful Lord of heaven and earth. If he was able to preserve Abraham's offspring in view of his *promise* of the Messiah, he will surely preserve us who are Abraham's children by virtue of sharing *in* the Messiah—we upon whom the ends of the ages have come; we who have obtained the inheritance of sons. Whatever our struggle of faith, our God and heavenly Father remains faithful, for he cannot deny himself (2 Tim. 2:13).

Chapter 2
Setting the Stage

Like every good story, the book of Esther begins by establishing a context. In this case, those contextual elements include the setting of the story and the introduction of a primary character in the story's movement and development. The setting for the Esther story is the city of Susa, capital of the Medo-Persian Empire and seat of the throne of King Ahasuerus (486–464 BC), who is introduced in the first verse of the book. Ahasuerus's kingdom, which extended from India to Ethiopia, also included the two houses of Israel (Israel and Judah), both the exiles who had returned to Jerusalem decades earlier and those who remained scattered throughout the Middle East.

Ahasuerus's role in the story is tied to both his reign and the kingdom he ruled. As the ruler of the vast Medo-Persian Empire, Ahasuerus held supreme authority, and that authority included his prerogative to impose and enforce royal edicts that would serve as binding law throughout the empire. At the same time, the king's power was held in check by an overarching law to which even he was subject. That law specified that no royal edict or decree could be withdrawn or overturned once it had been issued and written into law. Sovereign and subjects alike were forever bound by any such decree and that motivated the king, whoever he might be, to think long and hard before writing something into law. (Imagine the effect this would have on present-day governments!)

Thus, Ahasuerus's importance in the story lies primarily in his relationship to the Medo-Persian system of law, which itself is a central thematic element (ref. vv. 1:8, 13, 15, 19–20, 3:8, 14, 4:8, 11, 16, 8:13, 9:1, 13–14). Law plays a key role in the book in that it contributes to the story's rising tension and the interplay between the natural and supernatural. Because Medo-Persian law was irrevocable and unalterable (ref. 1:19; cf. also Dan. 6:1–15), it serves two important and related purposes in the narrative: First, it helps to create and reinforce the expectation of certain dreadful outcomes associated with various situations that arise in the story. But, even more importantly, it provides the single great obstacle to the remarkable outcomes that actually occur.

In other words, the permanent and unchangeable nature of Medo-Persian law builds tension in the story by appearing to ensure certain outcomes. It creates expectations as the story moves along, expectations connected with the events and circumstances the characters experience. In that way, the reader is distracted from the unseen presence and overruling power of the supernatural. Again, the genius of the book of Esther is that the story plays out on the two levels of the natural and supernatural. The narrative itself focuses on the natural and apparent—the people, motives, intentions, circumstances, and occurrences that make up the story. At the same time, the writer constructed it so that it also tells the greater supernatural "story" that runs in parallel behind the scenes; the ultimate story behind the surface story.

The Introduction of Ahasuerus (1:1–8)

The writer began by introducing King Ahasuerus, but only as a vehicle for arriving at the story's true starting place, which was the king's banquet. He described Ahasuerus's greatness to set the context for the extravagant celebration he organized in his own honor. In the third year of his reign, the king called for all his nobles, rulers, and military leaders to come to the capital city of Susa, so that he could amaze and impress them with the magnificence of his kingdom. Ahasuerus's personal greatness was reflected in the greatness of his dominion, which the writer highlighted by noting that 180 days—half of an entire year—were set aside to fully display it (1:3–4). The capstone of that presentation was a lavish, weeklong banquet for those in attendance (1:6–7). Producing such an extravagant event may not impress a modern American reader, but it would have left Ahasuerus's subjects (and ancient readers) awestruck.

As a side note, some interpret the text as indicating that Ahasuerus actually held *two* banquets, one for his nobles and military leaders and one for his subjects in the capital city. The NASB version suggests this interpretation. But it's also possible the writer was following the Hebrew practice of introducing a subject, digressing to provide explanation or background information, and then returning to pick up the subject again. If that's the case here, he introduced the topic of the banquet in verse 3 and then explained in the next verse that this feast concluded a six-month period during which the king spotlighted the splendor and riches of his kingdom. After that explanation, the writer turned his attention back to the banquet itself, describing its details and outcome, which was his real concern.

Whether there were two banquets or only one, Ahasuerus's design was to bring to a crescendo his display of the glory of his kingdom in the hope of leaving those in attendance in absolute awe. That same intent lay behind his decision to send for his queen on the climactic last day of the banquet (1:10–11).

The Banishment of Ahasuerus's Queen (1:9–22)

After six months of parading his splendor, power, and wealth to those who governed his kingdom in his name, Ahasuerus decided to bring his exhibition to a fitting climax by presenting to them one of the most splendid of his conquests, namely his beautiful wife, Vashti. But Vashti was a proud woman and refused to be displayed as one of her husband's trophies and testimonials to his greatness. Beyond that, she knew that the banquet guests, like the king himself, were full of wine (1:10), and she had every reason to expect that this would turn into an unpleasant and degrading experience. And so, when the king's eunuchs came to fetch her, Vashti sent them back with the reply that she would not answer his summons.

Ahasuerus's stunned reaction to this news was entirely predictable (1:12). He'd spent six months striving to impress his nobles and subjects with the greatness of his rule, only to have his *wife*—a mere

24

female whose royal status and life itself continued at his pleasure—snub his authority publicly in their presence. Vashti's open refusal told the banquet guests that their great king who wielded unchallenged authority over the world's largest empire couldn't command the submission of his own wife.

Ahasuerus responded to this outrage by immediately calling for his wise men—the seven princes who enjoyed preeminent status in his kingdom—to help him decide what to do with this defiant woman who'd publicly spurned and shamed him (1:13–15). The writer highlighted the counsel of one of the princes, a man named Memucan, who insisted that Vashti's offense reached beyond the king to all of the men in his kingdom. He argued that the news of her insubordination was going to spread like wildfire across the empire and her example as queen would embolden and encourage the same attitude and behavior in other women. Vashti's action had the potential to undermine the order and well-being of the entire kingdom, and so it was necessary that she be dealt with quickly and severely (1:16–18).

Memucan diagnosed the situation and provided his remedy: Ahasuerus needed to issue a royal edict formally deposing Vashti as queen and dismiss her from his presence. Moreover, this edict should be written into Medo-Persian law so as to establish a permanent, irrevocable statute that would discourage all future insubordination of wives toward their husbands (1:19–20). This counsel pleased the king and he proceeded to issue the edict and distribute it by letter throughout his empire (1:21–22). Her fate sealed by the supreme, unalterable authority of Medo-Persian law, Vashti was dispatched from the king's presence and stripped of her status as queen. The law put her in her place, and it threatened the same for any woman under its jurisdiction who attempted to set herself against her husband. By royal edict, every man was lord over his own house.

The writer's purpose in recording this episode had nothing per se to do with either Vashti's conduct or Ahasuerus's response. The reason for beginning his story this way is that it set the stage for introducing Esther and the critical role she was to play in the ensuing events. Vashti's deposition as queen left a vacuum in the king's house, and it was the need to fill that vacuum that provided the occasion and backdrop for Esther's entrance into the story.

The "laws of the Medes and Persians" determined Vashti's fate, and she does not appear again in the story. But her circumstance introduces the concept of Medo-Persian law, which becomes a crucial theme in the story's development. This form of law acts as an invincible force that no earthly power can overcome; as such, it stands behind another key theme in the Esther story, namely the *casting of the lot* (3:7, 9:24). In the ancient world, one would "cast the lot" in order to obtain an answer regarding a decision or future outcome (cf. Lev. 16:8; Josh. 18:1–10; Jonah 1:1–7; Mark 15:24). The idea is that the lot can see what human beings cannot, and so its judgment is ultimate and its answer is final.

Medo-Persian law resembled the lot in that, once decreed and enacted, there was no reversing it. It effectively "cast the lot" on behalf of all under its jurisdiction, sealing their future. Like Frankenstein's monster, it even overpowered the ruler who gave it life; everyone under its sway was subject to it. Medo-Persian law would soon cast the lot against Esther and her Jewish countrymen, and nothing under heaven would be able to change its decree. Once cast, the lot is fixed, and yet the Esther story underscores another power—an invisible, intangible one—that is able to work within the confines of the lot to bring about a different outcome.

The book of Esther highlights the truth that the lot cast by men—whether it takes the form of a ritual decision or an unchangeable law—is still subject to the One who reigns over all powers in earth and heaven (Prov. 16:33). The term, "lot," is *pur* in Hebrew, and it is the basis of the Jewish festival of *Purim* introduced at the end of the book (9:20–32). Each year at Purim, the Jewish people celebrate the Lord of the *pur*, the God who cast his lot for Abraham's offspring such that, through them and the "seed" to come from them, his blessing would flood the earth and all its families. The casting of *that* lot determined the fate of the whole world; every other lot, whatever its verdict, is bound by the Lord's *pur*. So the lot about to be cast against Esther, Mordecai, and their countrymen would not prevail. It would stand, but another lot would overcome it.

God's lot was at work in the events of the Esther story, but it looked beyond that time and circumstance to his ultimate goal for the entire world. When he "cast the lot" on behalf of Esther and her fellows Jews, he was casting it on behalf of all people and the entire cursed creation. And as his lot prevailed for the Jews in Esther's day, so it continues to prevail, though its power is unseen and undetected. And because it prevails, the Lord's *pur* ensures that everything under the sun has meaning and works toward the fulfillment of his purposes, even where this meaning and purpose elude human understanding.

Chapter 3
The New Queen of Medo-Persia

Vashti's insubordination resulted in her being stripped of her crown and banished from the king's presence. And because Ahasuerus acted by formal edict, there was no going back and no possibility of Vashti being restored; his decree was bound by the irrevocability of Medo-Persian law (1:19). For a time afterward, the king was content to rule without a queen, but soon his thoughts turned to finding a replacement for his beautiful former wife. And though he had a harem of concubines, he found no woman among them who was worthy of wearing the crown. But Ahasuerus ruled a vast empire, and his attendants encouraged him to appoint overseers in all of the provinces to locate and bring to Susa the most beautiful young virgins from which he might select a new queen. This counsel pleased the king, and he immediately issued the order (2:1–4).

The Introduction of Esther (2:5–14)

While Ahasuerus's servants were scouring his empire for suitable candidates to replace Vashti, a Jew named Mordecai was raising his cousin Hadassah (Esther) right under the king's nose in the capital city of Susa. The writer introduced Mordecai first, describing him as a descendant of the tribe of Benjamin. His forefathers, along with thousands of other Jews, had been taken captive from Jerusalem and Judah in 597 BC when the Babylonian king, Nebuchadnezzar, deposed King Jeconiah (Jehoiachin) and installed his uncle, Zedekiah, on the throne of Judah (2 Chron. 36:9–10). It's possible the writer described Mordecai this way simply to explain how he came to be living in the Persian capital city so far from the land of Israel. But it's much more likely he mentioned these details because of their significance in the history of Israel.

After David brought the Israelite kingdom to the fullness promised to Abraham (cf. Gen. 15:18–21, 22:15–17 with 1 Chron. 18:1–3 and 1 Kings 4:20–21), his failures as king initiated a period of decline that led to the division of his kingdom and finally the captivity of the two sub-kingdoms of Israel and Judah. David's kingdom was destroyed, but God's judgment went beyond that; during the reign of Jeconiah, David's descendant, God declared through the prophet Jeremiah that he was forever severing David's regal line: No descendant of Jeconiah ("Coniah") would ever sit on David's throne (Jer. 22:24–30).

Centuries of unfaithfulness and increasing idolatry provoked God to finally move against David's throne and kingdom, and he destroyed them through conquest and captivity. Jeremiah's prophecy was fulfilled when the Babylonian king, Nebuchadnezzar, deposed and exiled Jeconiah to Babylon and appointed his uncle Zedekiah to serve as his vassal king. Eleven more years, and nothing remained of the once-glorious Israelite kingdom (2 Chron. 36:9–21); what was once the envy of the nations had become an object of derision (Lamen. 1:1–8).

And so, to a Jew reading the book of Esther, Mordecai's circumstance meant more than merely an Israelite living outside the land of Canaan; it was a painful reminder of Israel's unfaithfulness to her Lord and the severe judgment it had incurred. After centuries of seeking the nation's repentance, even reducing David's kingdom to a shadow of its former glory, God finally brought the kingdom and its throne to an end. But more significant than the destruction of the Israelite kingdom was the implication for his larger purposes.

For God had chosen Abraham to be his instrument for restoring the fallen world; through Abraham, his blessing would go out to all of the earth's families. But this blessing wasn't going to come through Abraham himself, but the nation descended from him. The Creator's plan for the world was to be realized through *Israel*, the "seed" of Abraham. In God's design, Israel's faithfulness as his covenant son

(Exod. 4:22–23) would result in the world coming to know him in truth. For a son bears the likeness of his father, so that Israel's faithful life in the sight of the nations would testify to them of Israel's covenant Father—the God who is the Creator and God of all people. Thus, the nation's unfaithfulness amounted to its failure to fulfill its calling as Abraham's offspring. That failure, in turn, jeopardized God's covenant with Abraham, and so his plan to restore his cursed creation. Any Jew who knew the Scriptures would understand that Mordecai's presence in Susa was hugely significant, not just for Israel, but the whole world and the God who created it.

After introducing Mordecai, the writer turned his attention to Esther, describing her as being "beautiful of form and face" (2:7). This description left no doubt concerning where the story was going—the young Jewess, Hadassah, was going to be swept up in the king's search for a new queen, creating the expectation that she would soon wear the crown of Medo-Persia.

But if this were to happen, what would it mean for Esther's Jewish countrymen? From the beginning, God had called Israel to be a holy (separate) people and the northern ten tribes, who preceded Judah into exile, had long since abandoned this obligation, diluting and corrupting their Israelite identity through intermarriage with Gentiles. If Esther were joined in marriage to the Persian king, wouldn't this send a disastrous message to the other Israelite exiles scattered throughout his empire? Her disobedience would become known to all her fellow Jews, setting a precedent which, if followed by enough of them, could perhaps seal the end of Israel as the Lord's distinct covenant nation. Such concerns might escape the notice of contemporary readers, but not the original audience. They would have marveled at God's providential wisdom in using a Jewess's apparently defiling marriage to preserve the entire community of Jewish exiles.

The balance of this portion of the story details Esther's candidacy and her preparation under Hegai, the king's eunuch in charge of the harem of virgins. Esther was part of a large group of carefully selected young women, all of whom must have been striking in their beauty and poise. She was only one of many, but the writer was careful to distinguish her from all the others.

First of all, he noted her privileged favor with Hegai, who provided her with seven personal attendants, choice maids from the king's palace to care for her personal needs. So, also, Hegai exalted her to the leading place within the harem of candidates. Esther found special favor with Hegai, and so it would be with everyone she interacted with. The writer especially highlighted her distinction among the other women in describing her final preparation to appear before the king. Each lady was allowed to wear whatever jewelry or other adornments she believed would most effectively attract Ahasuerus's attention and win his favor (2:13). When her time came, Esther humbly deferred to Hegai's judgment. The text doesn't say how he advised her, but the writer's remark that she found favor with all who saw her suggests that Hegai recommended that she go before the king without any trappings or accessories and simply allow the aura of her modesty and natural beauty to win his heart (2:15).

Ahasuerus's Choice of Esther (2:15–18)

Hegai was deeply impressed with Esther and his instincts were spot on; when she appeared before the king he was completely taken by her. She captured his heart, and he knew right away that he'd found his new queen. After setting Vashti's crown on her head, Ahasuerus set about to honor and celebrate Queen Esther. Reminiscent of the festivities four years earlier, the king held a great banquet and appointed a holiday to be celebrated throughout all the provinces of his vast empire. This time, however, the purpose of the banquet wasn't to display and celebrate his own greatness; it was to pay tribute to the new queen of Medo-Persia. This was *Esther's* banquet (2:18).

From the time she came into the palace harem, Esther distinguished herself above all the other women. She was the center of attention, and yet a woman very much cloaked in secrecy. At Mordecai's request, Esther didn't reveal her Jewish identity to anyone, not even the king (2:10, 20). The writer didn't explain this, but the impression is that Mordecai believed Esther's well-being in the palace depended on her concealing her ethnicity. This, then, suggests that the Jews held a lowly and precarious place within Ahasuerus's kingdom. But whatever motivated Mordecai's instruction, coming events were about to reveal the wisdom of his counsel beyond what he imagined at that time. Behind Mordecai's judgment lay the wise, all-knowing design of divine providence—the overarching purpose of Mordecai's God.

The Threat on Ahasuerus's Life (2:19–23)

The effectual operation of a hidden providential hand is central to the development of the storyline and the second chapter ends with a providential incident that would be hugely important later on. Throughout the process leading to Esther's coronation, Mordecai had remained as close to her as he could, coming daily to the harem in order to find out how she was faring (2:11). And even after Esther was crowned queen, he continued to sit outside the palace, hoping to make contact with her. *Mordecai had no way of knowing it, but his loving concern for the cousin he'd raised as a daughter would make him party to a situation that would have enormous significance in the immediate future—not just for him and his cousin, but the entire Jewish nation under Persian rule.*

The writer noted that this incident occurred "when the virgins were gathered together the second time." This seems to locate it during the period when the king was still interviewing the harem of virgins. But two considerations argue against this: the first is that Mordecai is described as sitting at the king's gate (vv. 19, 21), and prior to Esther's coronation Mordecai came to inquire about her at the harem where she was staying. During that time, he had no reason to sit outside the king's quarters. But more importantly, the text states that Mordecai reported the incident in question to *Queen* Esther (2:22). And so the writer was most likely referring to a later time when the king was again seeking new concubines for his harem.

Mordecai continued his effort to stay in contact with Esther after she became queen, regularly coming to the palace and waiting outside the king's gate. On one such occasion, he became aware of a plot against Ahasuerus by two of his doorkeepers. It's not clear whether Mordecai overheard the two men talking or learned about the conspiracy in another way, but providence ensured that he was in the right place at the right time. So, also, Mordecai could have turned away, unconcerned about the pagan king who was ruling over his countrymen, but something moved him to get word to Esther so that she could warn Ahasuerus of the plot against him.

When the king learned of the conspiracy, he immediately launched an investigation. And discovering that the charges were true, he had the two conspirators hanged on a gallows. Most importantly to the events soon to transpire, the whole episode—including the fact that the conspiracy had been reported by a man named Mordecai—was made a matter of permanent record by being written into the Book of the Chronicles of the Medo-Persian kingdom (2:23). That seemingly insignificant action (much as Mordecai's regular practice of sitting outside the king's gate) would prove critical in the days ahead. Divine providence would afford it a crucial place in a whole series of outcomes whose ultimate importance reaches from the Creator's eternal counsel to the consummate glory of the new heavens and earth.

Chapter 4
The Plot against the Jews

The writer used Ahasuerus's six-month celebration as the occasion to introduce Mordecai and Esther and her ascension to the throne. So the events of chapter two provide the springboard for Haman's introduction into the narrative, "After these things, King Ahasuerus promoted Haman..." The author's timing was intentional—Mordecai's and Esther's relation to the king needed to be established before Haman came into the picture because of how these four individuals play against one another in the story's development and outcome.

The Introduction of Haman (3:1)

In contrast to the other two main characters, the man, Haman, enters the story abruptly. The writer says nothing about his life or his background in Ahasuerus's service and only identifies him as an *Agagite*. To a Jewish reader, this description linked Haman with Agag—a name (or possibly a title) ascribed in the Old Testament to two kings of the Amalekite people (ref. Num. 24:7; 1 Sam. 15:8). The Jewish author was certainly aware of this, and his intent in establishing this connection becomes evident in the light of biblical history.

Haman's connection with Agag links him with Amalek, the forefather of the Amalekite nation. Amalek was the grandson of Esau, Jacob's brother, and he went on to become one of the princes of Edom (ref. Gen. 36:10–16). As Esau represented opposition to God's covenant and his covenant people, so the Amalekite nation descended from him epitomized the enemies of Israel, and therefore the enemies of Israel's God. The Amalekites fought against

Israel during their wilderness wanderings (Exod. 17:8–16; Deut. 25:17–19) and resisted their possession of the land of Canaan (Num. 13:25–31; Judg. 3:1–14, 6:1–6).

An episode recorded in 1 Samuel 15 provides further insight into the relationship between Israel and the Amalekites. In that context, Agag, the king of the Amalekites, was the focal point in a test of Israel's obedience to Yahweh (*Yahweh* is God's covenant name). After defeating the Amalekites in battle (1 Sam. 14:47–48), God commanded King Saul to go out against them again, and this time utterly destroy them and everything belonging to them (cf. 1 Sam. 15:2–3 with Exod. 17:8–16). But Saul decided to hold back the choicest items among the spoil and spare Agag so that he could parade him before Israel as his trophy of victory. This act of disobedience, together with Saul's previous violation of the priesthood (1 Sam. 13:5–14), cost him the throne of Israel. The Lord's anointed king willfully disobeyed his command, and it was Samuel, his prophet and judge, who had to step up and carry out his will against Amalek.

The Old Testament scriptures present the house of Amalek as the counterpart of the house of Israel. As the latter is the national extension of *Jacob* (Israel), so the former is the extension of *Esau*. And so, by linking Haman with Agag and the Amalekite nation, the writer was suggesting to his readers that there will be *covenantal* implications to Haman's role in the story. *Before anything else is known about Haman or he has made any contribution to the narrative, the reader—whom the author assumes understands the larger story of Israel's history—already senses what is coming.* The writer wanted his readers to anticipate from the outset what he'd soon make clear: Haman would prove to be an avowed enemy of Abraham's covenant household; like Agag, Amalek, and Esau before him, he was a son in the line of the serpent's seed (ref. again Gen. 3:15).

Mordecai's Conflict with Haman (3:2–5)

The writer's description of Haman suggested that a threat to the covenant people stood on the horizon, and he laid the foundation for that threat in the circumstance of Haman's promotion.

Again, the text gives no indication of Haman's previous status or role in Ahasuerus's administration; the author was only concerned to relate his new place of preeminence among the king's nobles. Other than Ahasuerus himself, no one in the vast Medo-Persian kingdom was now greater than Haman. His prestige and authority were second only to the king (3:1), and it was that newly-granted status that enabled the coming conflict.

Haman's promotion afforded him great distinction, and Ahasuerus demanded that all his subjects acknowledge it by bowing down and paying homage to Haman whenever he was in their presence. But Mordecai openly refused to honor this command, even after repeated challenges by the king's servants (3:2–3). The reason Mordecai gave for his refusal was that he was a Jew (3:4a). The writer didn't explain this, but the implication is that Mordecai viewed this particular homage as a kind of *idolatry*. Israelites were perfectly willing to bow before a ruler or authority as a gesture of honor and submission (cf. 1 Sam. 24:8; 2 Sam. 1:1–2, 9:6–8, 14:4–5, 21–22; 1 Kings 1:15–16), suggesting that Mordecai believed he was being asked to offer a kind of veneration that belongs only to God. It also seems that Haman required this veneration beyond what Ahasuerus commanded. Two things point in this direction: First, it was common practice in ancient cultures—including Persia—for rulers to regard themselves as divine and therefore proper objects of worship. Assuming Ahasuerus viewed himself this way, it's unlikely he'd call for the veneration of his subordinate, thus diminishing his own unique status in the eyes of his subjects. Haman's personality also supports the idea that he, not the king, demanded this sort of recognition. The author characterizes him as fiercely arrogant, a man who was calculating and ruthless in his aspirations, willing even to exploit the king himself in order to achieve his ends.

Whatever the case, Mordecai was resolute, and Ahasuerus's servants soon realized that there was nothing they could do to convince him to comply. Apparently fearing Haman's retribution, they went to him to explain Mordecai's reason for refusing to pay homage. The text suggests they were hopeful that Haman would accept Mordecai's behavior once he learned of his Jewish identity (3:4b).

He would then understand that Mordecai intended no dishonor or disrespect but was simply honoring a religious custom peculiar to the Israelite people.

But their hope was not realized; when Haman heard their explanation, he became enraged (3:5). Not only was Mordecai's ethnicity not an acceptable reason for his defiance, it added insult to injury. It wasn't a Persian who refused to bow to him, but a *Jew*—a man who was part of a byword nation, a despised and impotent people, which Persia had ruled for nearly a century. Who did this Jew think he was to refuse to bow to his lord, a man who was second only to Ahasuerus himself, the great king whose dominion embraced half the civilized world including the long-subjugated Jewish nations of Israel and Judah?

Haman's Conspiracy Against the Jews (3:6–15)

Haman's fury burned against Mordecai, but he realized he had a bigger problem. If this Jew's identity really was the reason for his insolence, Haman could expect the same response from all of his countrymen. Even more, Mordecai's example would surely embolden others. The thought of Jews across the kingdom mocking and insulting him in this way was more than Haman could bear, and he determined at that moment that he wouldn't rest until he had seen the destruction of all of the Jews under Ahasuerus's reign (3:6).

Haman was pompous and driven, but he wasn't stupid or impetuous. He realized his goal was no small feat, and that it would never be achieved without the king's approval and support. And so he sought out the diviners of the kingdom to "cast the lot" on his behalf in order to determine what, if any, day in the future would yield success for his plan. (Some English versions are misleading; the NIV, NAB, and NKJV capture the meaning of the text). The lot was cast, and it gave its answer—the Jews were to be destroyed on the thirteenth day of the month, eleven months hence (3:7).

The writer introduced the concept of the lot (*pur*) at this point in the story, and then there's no mention of it again until the end where it becomes a major theme (ref. 9:24–32). This approach highlights one of the key ironies in the story—at its first appearance, the lot symbolizes the certain doom of the Jewish people; in the closing summary, the lot appears in its plural form, *purim*, in reference to the annual celebration by which the Jews commemorated their deliverance and preservation. The first lot sealed their destruction, but a second lot emerged later that counteracted the first one. Thus, the lot is a key thematic element, forming an *inclusio*[2] that frames the entire story.

The concept of the *pur* acts as an inclusio in the Esther story, and it serves as a metaphor for divine promise as upheld and advanced by God's providential oversight. The lot was cast to determine a course of action, the implication being that it has insight into future outcomes; the lot knows what lies ahead and so is able to reveal to the inquirer how he should proceed. God's promise is like the lot in that it also knows the future and its outcomes and so provides the one who possesses it with direction and sure confidence as he plans his course. But whereas the lot cast by men supposedly sees the future, God's promise knows the future because it determines it.

This metaphorical relationship helps clarify the shift from the singular, *pur*, at the beginning of the story to the plural, *purim*, at the end. The Jews' fate was sealed when Haman received the "word" of the lot. The lot enabled him to peer into the future, and he set himself to act accordingly. But, again, as the story unfolds, it will become evident that *another* lot exists—a lot distinguished from its counterpart in two critically important ways: First of all, the second *pur* is the one that speaks the truth and is therefore vindicated when the future finally presents itself. Secondly, the first lot served its truthful counterpart in that it provided the delay that enabled the outcome determined by the latter.

Emboldened by what the lot revealed to him, Haman went to Ahasuerus to seek his approval and authorization for his genocidal plan. His argument to the king was clever and persuasive—there

---

2   *Inclusio* is a literary device used often in the Scriptures. It consists of a word, phrase, or idea that introduces and concludes a passage. An *inclusio* highlights a passage by bracketing it like bookends, but it also provides insight into the passage's meaning or significance.

existed within the kingdom a group of foreign troublemakers who continued to cling to their own obscure laws and refused to submit to the laws of Medo-Persia. They had demonstrated that they were never going to comply with the king's directives, and for this reason, it was unwise and even dangerous to allow them to remain alive (3:8).

Haman was confident that Ahasuerus would consider criminal insubordination sufficient ground for eradicating the Jews, but he also anticipated the king's concern about the logistics and expense of carrying out such an ambitious plan. The Jews were scattered across the far reaches of the empire, so that identifying and killing all of them would require a great deal of coordination, manpower, and money. Haman intercepted this probable objection by offering to donate ten thousand talents of silver toward the cause (much of which he hoped to regain through plunder). This would fully fund the enterprise with plenty left to build up the reserves of the king's treasury (3:9).

Hoping that his proposition would prove agreeable to Ahasuerus, Haman petitioned him, not merely for authorization, but for a *decree*. He knew that the one he needed to authorize his plan could also suspend or annul it. But even Ahasuerus was subject to the irrevocable decrees of Medo-Persian law; if he could extract a formal edict from the king, then any future remorse or reconsideration would be meaningless; nothing could derail his design. Haman had Ahasuerus right where he wanted him, and he wasn't about to let go until he had sealed the outcome he sought.

Ahasuerus was persuaded by Haman's arguments and, in a gesture delegating his royal authority to compose and distribute the decree, the king removed his signet ring and gave it to Haman, "the Agagite, the enemy of the Jews" (3:10). That simple designation fully exposed the significance of Haman's identity—he had become an Agagite indeed, continuing the long-standing Amalekite opposition to Israel, which conflict began nearly fifteen hundred years earlier with the two twins Jacob and Esau (Gen. 25:19–26). Not long before, Haman had given little or no thought to the Israelites scattered throughout the kingdom; now, he was sworn to their complete destruction. Haman's transformation into the avowed "enemy of the Jews," viewed in light of the lot's insight and the irrevocable edict about to be issued, signals to the reader that inescapable doom now awaited the Hebrew people; nothing, it seems, would be able to prevent their annihilation.

Ahasuerus authorized Haman to construct this decree and, when it was complete, copies were sent throughout the empire. The decree ordered that eleven months hence, on the thirteenth day of the twelfth month, the authorities in every province were to rise up against the Hebrews under their jurisdiction and put them to death in a great slaughter. In one day, all Jews were to be purged from the vast Medo-Persian Empire and their property seized (3:11–14).

His mission accomplished, Haman joined the king in a time of triumphal celebration. But while they celebrated, all around them shock and confusion were spreading through the city (3:15). Thus, the scene ends on a note of pointed contrast; there, at the epicenter of the shockwave that was already moving across the empire, two men toasted their triumph while their subjects were reeling. And yet, these contrasting responses reflected the very same confidence—Haman's decree, empowered by the inviolability of Medo-Persian law, would surely achieve its objective.

The news of Ahasuerus's edict raced across the empire, and in every place its words were read it brought a visceral response from those who heard. Interestingly, the writer first mentioned the confused response of the people of Susa. This is significant because Susa was the capital of the empire, and most of its residents would have been Persian. This raises two questions—why did a decree concerning the Jews shock Susa's Persian population? And why would the author take note of the city's response before addressing the Jews' reaction?

The first question is reasonably answered by the fact that the edict called for the slaughter of every Jew under Persian rule over the course of a single day (ref. 8:11). How could that not provoke astonishment and confusion? But the text suggests more than that; it seems the writer intended to convey that *this sort of decree had no precedent*. Susa's citizens were shocked because they had never before seen such an edict calling for the complete annihilation of an entire race of people. Ancient empires had no problem with unspeakable brutality, but they shed blood for the sake of conquest, expansion, and wealth, not genocide.

This also helps to explain why the author chose to address the Gentile response first. By intimating that this sort of genocide was unprecedented in the history of the Medo-Persian Empire—an empire well acquainted with massive and bloody military campaigns, he puts in perspective the scope and severity of this coming purge. If Ahasuerus's Persian subjects were mortified at what had been decreed for the Jews, how would the Jews themselves react? The Gentile reaction, then, sets the stage for the intense Jewish response. And taken together, the reaction of both groups highlights the gravity of the situation and heightens the story's tone of despair.

The Jews' Response to the Decree (4:1–5)

The writer began with Mordecai's reaction to the edict and then mirrored that reaction in his countrymen throughout the empire. Everywhere the news spread, it was met with loud and bitter wailing and the donning of sackcloth and ashes. So also the Jews responded with *fasting* (4:3), which itself makes an important contribution to the story. The reason is that fasting was an aspect of the Jews' interaction with God, particularly as they sought his forgiveness or merciful intervention (cf. 1 Sam. 7:1–6; 1 Kings 21:18ff; Ezra 8:21ff). The Day of Atonement (Yom Kippur) provides a good case in point. God's prescription for Yom Kippur didn't specify fasting, but the sons of Israel fasted nonetheless. They did so because the Lord directed them to prepare for that most holy day by denying themselves—by "bringing their souls low" before him (Lev. 23:27), and such a focused and contrite state of mind naturally tends to express itself in fasting.

And so, by pointing out the Jews' fasting, the writer was reinforcing the story's perspective that the God who is unmentioned (unmentioned because he had apparently abandoned his people in their exile) was not absent. They fasted in the hope that their God would take notice of their plight and intervene—not merely as an act of mercy, but of *faithfulness*. For their God was the covenant God of

41

Abraham, Isaac, and Jacob, the God who had promised to preserve and establish his covenant people, come what may. Abraham's children fasted in the hope that their God would remember them and show himself faithful to his word.

Even within the sheltered world of the king's palace, Esther could not escape the crisis, and her attendants soon brought her word of what her new husband had decreed. At this point, however, it seems she didn't have a clear sense of what all this meant. She was anguished at the news, but also sent Mordecai new clothes to replace his sackcloth. This action suggests that she didn't understand the extent of the king's edict, a suggestion which the writer affirms. When Mordecai refused her gift, she sent Hathach, her personal male attendant, to find out from him what this decree was all about and why it had put him in such a state of distress (4:4–6).

Mordecai's Plea (4:6–14)

Hathach found Mordecai in the city square and relayed Esther's concerns and questions. Mordecai sent him back to her with a copy of the king's edict along with the explanation that this decreed genocide of the Jewish people was the fruit of an evil scheme concocted by Haman—a scheme Mordecai himself was partially responsible for. Most importantly, he directed the servant to convey his charge to Esther that she go in to the king and plead for the lives of her people (4:6–8).

Hathach returned to Esther, showed her the edict, and relayed Mordecai's words to her. She responded by sending the eunuch back to her cousin to inform him that she shared his agony over this turn of events, but he wrongly presumed that she had a privileged standing or unique influence with Ahasuerus. While Medo-Persian law permitted anyone to seek an audience with the king, no one—not even the queen herself—could simply march into his presence without permission. Anyone who dared to do so (unless by chance he caught the king at a moment of unusual generosity) would find his impudence rewarded with death. Furthermore, the king had not called for her for the past month, and so she had no reason to believe he would grant her an audience (4:9–12). And even if he did, this matter involved Haman, a man whom he'd just exalted to the head of his kingdom.

When Mordecai received Esther's message, he sent back his reply, pointing out the implication of her own words—the very fact that she had no special standing with the king meant that she would not be exempted from the coming destruction. She, too, was a Jew and would surely receive the same sentence as her countrymen; death was going to confront her whether or not she chose to remain silent. At the same time, she must not think that the fate of her people rested upon her decision. Should she fail to act, *the Jews would nonetheless obtain relief in the form of deliverance from another place* (4:14a).

As he did before, but this time in explicit fashion, the writer provided a glimpse into his perspective and purpose in composing his account. Some might observe that including this statement in the narrative was pointless since the outcome of this crisis had already occurred at the time of the writing (ref. 10:2). But the author was not merely stating the obvious; he recorded Mordecai's insight in order to draw attention to the fact that forces and concerns were at work behind the events playing out day-to-day. The story he was telling goes far beyond what meets the eye.

The course of events dictated by the decree was not inevitable, regardless of how things appeared. Yes, Esther had a unique opportunity and responsibility to plead for her people, but her actions would not determine the outcome. Mordecai was convinced that Haman's plan would fail and deliverance would come, if not through Esther's intervention, then by some other instrument, natural or supernatural. The writer didn't explain Mordecai's confidence because he didn't need to. He wrote for a Jewish audience, and every Jew understood that God's design for the world, centered in Israel's Messiah, depended upon the continuance of the covenant household of Israel. *The annihilation of the Jewish people would mean the failure of God's promises and that was beyond the realm of possibility.*

Mordecai was confident that Haman's plan wouldn't succeed in the ultimate sense, but this didn't mean no Jews would die. Part of Mordecai's message to Esther was a warning that, should she fail to act, she and her father's household would perish (4:14). This statement has two reasonable interpretations. The first is that Mordecai was speaking of *divine judgment*—God would still bring deliverance even if Esther refused to intervene, but she'd incur a severe penalty for abandoning her people in their hour of need. The Israelite people would survive, but not her and her household. The second, and arguably better interpretation, is that Mordecai was predicting a *limited deliverance*. God would see to it that Haman's attempt at genocide didn't succeed, but countless Jews could still be slaughtered. And given Esther's situation, she would surely be among them.

Mordecai was no fool; he may or may not have been aware of the irrevocability of Ahasuerus's decree, but he knew first-hand Haman's implacable hatred. With such a man at the helm, it was unthinkable that no Jewish blood was going to be spilled. In Haman's hand, the king's edict would surely see some Jews murdered, and certainly Esther and her family among them. For it was Mordecai's insubordination that provoked Haman's rage and murderous course; even if Haman wasn't able to accomplish his goal of eradicating every Jew in the empire, he'd make sure that Mordecai fell under the sword. And once Esther was discovered to be his relative, there was no doubt that she'd meet the same end. Haman would insist on it, and Ahasuerus was bound by his own decree. Even his great love for Esther couldn't set it aside.

Esther's Promise (4:15–17)

When Esther received this final message from Mordecai, she sent her servant back to him one last time. She would present herself to the king as he'd asked, but she required something of him. *She would not go before Ahasuerus except in solidarity with her people.* All the Jews in Susa must come together in a solemn fast, eating and drinking nothing for the next three days and nights. Though she couldn't join them personally, she, too, would fast along with her maidservants. If her people agreed to stand together with her in this way, Esther would do as Mordecai asked. According to his word, she would trust herself once again to an unseen and unpredictable providence (4:14b). If she was appointed to perish, then perish she would.

The implication, again, is that this fast was to be a time of humble, unceasing petition to God. But if this is the case, why was the writer so careful not to mention *prayer* as the point of the fast, either here or in the previous passage (ref. 4:3)? The simple answer is that the writer had determined not to mention God in his account. He *intimated* God's presence and preserving hand (ref. 4:14, 6:13, 9:1), but any mention of prayer to him would have openly brought him into the story.

Chapter 5
The Turning of the Lot—Mordecai and Haman

Chapter five begins the second major section of the book. The first three chapters show how the threat to the Jews came about, while chapters 5–9 chronicle their victory over it. The fourth chapter forms the hinge between those two sections by transitioning the story's focus from impending and sure destruction to triumphal deliverance. The writer accomplished this by means of a dialogue between Mordecai and Esther, which culminated with her agreeing to go before the king on behalf of her people. These two characters share center stage, but as representing the larger community of Jewish exiles under Ahasuerus's dominion. Mordecai exhorted Esther to approach the king for the sake of their countrymen and she made her decision in solidarity with them. She joined them in a three-day fast in which they together sought the intervening mercy of their God. This collective fasting mirrors the collective mourning that accompanied the news of the king's decree (ref. 4:3, 16), and the two episodes form another *inclusio* having its focal point in Mordecai's declaration of confident faith in verse 4:14a. That structure is an important interpretive key, for it provides a clue as to how seemingly inescapable destruction was going to give way to deliverance: *Triumph was certain because Israel's God never forgets or forsakes his promise.*

Whatever the threat or obstacle, God would indeed fulfill his promise to Eve of a conquering seed; his decree overrules any and every human decree. And his long-standing decree meant that Abraham's covenant descendants—the people chosen to give birth to the promised seed—would endure throughout their generations, whatever plight might befall them. God's faithful preservation of his covenant people in view of the coming deliverer is a central theme that binds together the entire Old Testament narrative, and so it is in the book of Esther. This theme comes to the forefront in the Esther story in two distinct ways. The first is the most obvious, which is the astonishing deliverance of the entire community of Jewish exiles. The second is personal rather than collective. It takes the form of *a story within the story*, a story whose role is to predict and promise the wider deliverance. It is the story of Mordecai's triumph over Haman. As Haman embodied the human threat (and ultimately the satanic threat) to God's covenant people, so Mordecai epitomized that people. In this way, Mordecai's triumph in his personal conflict with Haman (5:1–8:2) prefigured his countrymen's later triumph over those who rose up against them because of Haman's decree (8:3–9:16).

Esther's First Banquet (5:1–8)

Mordecai honored Esther's request, and the story implies that the Jews of Susa joined her as she fasted and prayed in preparation to appear before her husband. The writer said nothing more about those three days, but the first verses of chapter 5 show that Esther formulated a plan during her fast. She determined that, if the king extended the scepter to her and allowed her to approach him, she would not mention the subject of the decree at that time. Ahasuerus would be seated on his throne (5:1) with attendants around him and Esther knew that confronting him in that setting would put him in an awkward position and jeopardize a favorable response. Instead, she would request the king's presence at a banquet later that day. Perhaps in that setting, and with Haman present to answer for his actions, the king would grant her petition.

When the three days of fasting were completed, Esther went before Ahasuerus and, as she'd hoped, he extended his scepter and called her to approach him. Knowing that only a great burden would lead her to risk coming before him unsummoned, the king immediately asked her what was troubling her and pledged to honor her request. (The expression, "even to half of the kingdom," emphasizes the king's willingness to give her whatever she desired.) Esther responded that she desired his and Haman's presence that day at a banquet she had prepared in his honor. Ahasuerus heartily agreed to her request and sent servants to retrieve Haman to join them (5:1–5).

At the banquet, the king again affirmed that he was prepared to give Esther whatever she desired (5:6). Perhaps she had told him earlier that she would make an additional request at that time, or he may simply have sensed that she was still preoccupied. Either way, Ahasuerus knew that there was more on her mind than the banquet. Esther's response was the same as before—she asked that he and Haman attend a second banquet to be held the following day. If they would honor this request, she promised that she would at that time divulge the burden on her heart (5:8).

The writer presented Haman as a silent observer to the exchange between Ahasuerus and Esther, but he's actually the central character in the scene. This part of the story is concerned with his fate, and this first banquet played a key role in setting the stage. Esther's plan played on Haman's fierce pride, and it was precisely that pride that would serve his downfall. He was an arrogant and self-centered man and likely paid no attention to the king's conversation with Esther until he heard her request his presence at a second banquet the next day. *That* he took notice of, and he left for home that day exulting in the sense of his own greatness and flooded with self-satisfaction. Of all the nobles and rulers in Ahasuerus's immense kingdom, only he had been invited to spend two evenings feasting with the king. Even more, the king hadn't issued the invitation, *Esther* had. If his preeminent status with the great King Ahasuerus weren't enough, he'd now also won the affection of his beloved queen. Who else in the whole of the kingdom could make that claim?

Haman's Conspiracy and Humiliation (5:9–6:14)

But Haman's triumphal self-celebration was to be short-lived; no sooner did he leave the banquet than he was confronted once again with the high-handed defiance of that troublesome thorn Mordecai. When Haman encountered him at the king's gate, his elation instantly gave way to indignation. Who did this loathsome Jew think he was? He wasn't dishonoring just any nobleman, but *Haman*, the man second only to Ahasuerus himself, the man whom even the king and his queen recognized and honored (5:9). But Haman controlled his anger, perhaps by reminding himself that he would yet have his due; his day of vengeance was coming, and the royal decree ensured that nothing would stop it.

Haman managed to restrain himself when Mordecai snubbed him, but he was deeply agitated in his spirit. Like all grandiose men, it was hugely important to him that everyone around him recognize and acknowledge the greatness he saw in himself. Mordecai not only insulted and dishonored him, he had "rained on his parade," and Haman was eager to have his glory reaffirmed, both in his own mind and in the esteem of others. And so, as soon as he arrived home, Haman called together his wife and friends in order to rehearse with them all of his excellencies and great accomplishments (5:11–12).

Haman was wealthy, successful, and incredibly powerful. He had secured for himself a place of unique authority in Ahasuerus's kingdom and was answerable only to the king himself. Even Queen Esther recognized and celebrated his greatness. Furthermore, his greatness would endure beyond him; he had been blessed with numerous sons to carry on his legacy after his death. And yet, for all that, discontentment gnawed at him because there was something he lacked that was like a splinter in his mind. There was a man out there in the street—a worthless Jew no less—who refused to give him the recognition and reverence he was due, and it was tormenting him (5:13).

Haman's wife and friends listened to his pained confession and then gave him exactly the sort of counsel one would expect—why would you subject yourself to this sort of treatment? You are Haman, second only to the king, and this man Mordecai is nothing—he is a lowly, contemptible Jew. There's absolutely no reason for you to suffer such defiance and disrespect. You have Ahasuerus's favor and so needn't wait for the decreed day of vengeance. Order gallows to be built tonight, and then tomorrow you can get the king's permission to have Mordecai hanged on it in the sight of all the people. That will take care of this problem and ensure that no one will dare to follow his example. Then, with this obnoxious Jew out of the picture, you'll be able to go with an unburdened and happy heart to Esther's second banquet. This advice was music to Haman's ears, and he immediately set about having the gallows constructed (5:14).

At this point, the writer immediately shifted the scene from Haman's home to the king's bedchamber (6:1). While Haman and his wife and guests were toasting their plan and workmen were busy gathering materials and building the gallows, Ahasuerus was restless in his bed. Unable to sleep, he decided that perhaps some reading from the official chronicles would help settle his mind, and so he called for a servant to get the book and read to him.

Ancient kings—including Israelite kings—typically kept elaborate accounts of their reign and accomplishments (ref. 1 Kings 11:41, 14:29, 15:7, 23, 31, 16:5, etc.). These records had national significance, but also were an important part of a king's legacy and ensured the immortality of his name and exploits. Ahasuerus evidently hoped that rehearsing the history of his reign would still the unrest robbing him of sleep. As his servant read from the book, he came upon the account of the conspiracy against the king's life and the fact that a man named Mordecai had exposed the plot and averted his assassination (ref. 2:21–23). That prompted Ahasuerus to ask whether this man's noble deed had been properly acknowledged and rewarded and the servant responded that nothing had been done for him (6:1–3).

When the morning dawned, and even as the king was discussing Mordecai and the best way to reward his loyalty, Haman arrived at the palace with the intent of getting the king's permission to have him hanged (6:4). In this way, this master storyteller brought his story to a high point of ironic tension—*the two most powerful men in the Medo-Persian Empire were poised to engage each other regarding the same individual, but with diametrically opposed agendas entirely unknown to the other.* Ahasuerus was committed to honoring and exalting Mordecai; Haman was bent on executing him in open humiliation.

A crucial feature of this development in the story is that it was the result of a natural sequence of events. There was nothing supernatural about it; indeed, the unmentioned, silent God played no discernible role in the circumstances leading up to that encounter in the palace. Simple, everyday—and apparently *chance*—occurrences brought Mordecai's fate to this crossroad. At the same time, his circumstance had significance far beyond him. What Mordecai faced with Haman, all of his fellow Jews faced, including Queen Esther. Mordecai stood in solidarity with his people, and the writer wanted his audience to see Mordecai's crisis as the crisis of the entire Israelite nation under Ahasuerus's rule. What befell him would somehow be reflected in their own fate.

The author brilliantly crafted his story so that it spotlights the hidden operation of divine providence while never mentioning it or giving any direct indication that God is at work. In this particular context, he brought together two separate streams of providential circumstances, each having an expected outcome for Mordecai that contradicts and excludes the other. In this way, the reader is left wondering which circumstance would prevail, the one bringing Mordecai's honor or his death.

With notable comedic flair, the writer drew upon Ahasuerus and Haman's unawareness of each other's agenda to bring the tension to its first point of resolution. The vehicle for that resolution was the king's question to Haman, "What is to be done for the man whom the king desires to honor?" Being the sort of man he was, Haman, of course, concluded that Ahasuerus was referring to him (6:6). After all, who else could he possibly have in mind? And since he was to be the object of this honor, Haman naturally called for a grandiose reward—the king should display this man's greatness by clothing him in his own royal robe, leading him through the square on his own horse bearing the royal crest and proclaiming his honored status to all onlookers (6:7–9).

This counsel pleased Ahasuerus, and he immediately commissioned Haman to do *on behalf of Mordecai* all that he had recommended. Haman had come before the king in smug confidence that this day would see the end of the man he so despised, and now he was being commanded to dress that man in the king's own garments, lead him on the king's horse before the people of Susa and personally proclaim his praises on the king's behalf! *Haman had fully expected to put Mordecai on display in Susa that day, but in degrading agony at the end of a rope. Never could he have imagined that **he** would be at the end of the rope, putting Mordecai on display by leading him through the city in triumphal procession.*

If Haman was distraught the night before, he was now absolutely dejected. Not only had his own words humiliated him by placing him in the position of a lowly servant in the sight of those under his authority—people who ought to be honoring him, this humiliation was for the sake of Mordecai's exaltation. It wasn't another man, but his own counsel that was forcing him to publicly extol the one person he hated above all others, and that in the name of the king himself, "Thus it shall be done to the man whom the king desires to honor." It was clear now that there was no possibility his plan for Mordecai would come to pass. How everything had changed in a matter of moments!

In this way, the writer hinted to his readers that the tide of circumstance was beginning to turn—Haman's preeminence was being eclipsed as Mordecai's esteem with the king and his subjects was on the rise. It wasn't simply that Mordecai had escaped the hangman's noose; providence was moving him toward triumph over Haman himself. Notably, the narrator doesn't make this observation. Rather, he let Haman's own wife and close friends (whom he here intentionally designated "wise men") make it for him (6:13). The night before they'd counseled Haman from the vantage point of his preeminence (ref. again 5:14); now their perspective was completely reversed. They detected in this new development the beginning of a shift in fortunes.

Haman's wife and friends sensed that he had begun to fall before Mordecai, and, most importantly, *they attributed this remarkable turn of events to the fact that Mordecai was of "the seed of the Jews."* Although some versions give the impression that they were unsure of Mordecai's Jewish identity—"*If* Mordecai is of Jewish origin..." (NASB), the text shows they were fully aware that he was a Jew (ref.

5:11–14). Their counsel is better rendered, "*Inasmuch as* Mordecai is of Jewish origin, you will not overcome him…"

Just the day before, Haman's wife and counselors had seen only a powerless Jew, and so advised him to simply put an end to Mordecai. Now, having witnessed a stunning reversal, they warned Haman that powerful providential forces were working on Mordecai's behalf, and there would be no halting or reversing this trend. Haman would not be able to prevail against this Jew; rather, in the end, he would find himself cast down before him.

The insight of Haman's counselors was all the more profound in the light of what the conflict between Haman and Mordecai represented. Again, their personal conflict was a picture of the larger struggle between the Jews and the Persian power now poised to destroy them. And beyond that, it pointed to the perpetual struggle between the serpent and his seed and Eve and her seed (ref. again Gen. 3:15). Obviously, Haman's advisors weren't aware of this backstory, but they sensed that some divine power was acting on Mordecai's behalf and so, it seemed, on behalf of all the Jews. They reasoned that it was because Mordecai was of Jewish origin ("from the seed of the Jews") that Haman was going to fall before him. And if they were right, didn't it follow that all of his Jewish countrymen would enjoy the same divine protection and ultimate triumph?

Thus, the writer ingeniously accomplished two things with this scene: First, he highlighted the certainty of Mordecai's deliverance and exaltation by putting the pronouncement of it in the mouths of his enemies. The very persons who'd confidently called for Mordecai's death were now convinced that the future held something very different for him. Secondly, the writer used their prediction to anticipate what lay ahead for Mordecai's countrymen. Sharing the Jewish ethnicity that was the reason for his triumph, they could expect the same fate at the hand of the same power. This is exactly what the story will disclose in the coming chapters.

The storyline in the book of Esther is woven together like a well-designed fabric. It traces out numerous providential circumstances that, while independent of one another, work together to bring about unexpected, even ironic outcomes. In the present situation involving Haman and Mordecai, one of the absolutely critical ones was Esther's seemingly random decision to withhold her petition from the king until the second banquet (ref. again 5:8). The text doesn't explain her delay, which gives the impression that it made no difference one way or the other. But in fact, it was pivotal, for if Esther had disclosed her request to Ahasuerus at the first banquet, the key events of 5:9–6:12 would not have occurred. Most importantly, the king wouldn't have been aware of Mordecai's unrewarded loyalty, so almost certainly he'd have viewed Esther's request differently (ref. 6:1–3).

Esther's Second Banquet (7:1–8)

Chapter seven chronicles Haman's undoing and death and thus records the fulfillment of the prediction made by his wife and friends. So, also, his demise completed what began with Mordecai's exaltation at his expense (6:10–11). As implied by that episode, Haman would indeed "fall," but, most importantly, he was to fall *before Mordecai*; Haman's downfall was to be accompanied by Mordecai's ascension. The astonishing reversal of the lots of these two men is the focus of this part of the story (7:1–8:2), and the writer underscores it by saturating the passage with irony. In various ways and through various means, things are most unexpectedly "turned on their head."

The chapter begins with Esther's second banquet, which Haman seemingly had forgotten about. He'd been thrilled to receive Esther's invitation, but the day's circumstances had pushed it from his mind. Indeed, he was still wrestling with the words of his wife and friends when Ahasuerus's servants arrived to escort him. Apparently, he was already late and likely would have missed the banquet altogether if the king hadn't fetched him. The writer introduced this second banquet as a virtual repetition of the first one, including the king's question to Esther and his pledge to give her whatever she wanted (7:2, cf. 5:6). By presenting the two banquets in this way, the writer effectively spotlighted the one crucial difference between them—the promise Esther made at the first banquet she honored at the second one, answering the king's question by making her request.

Esther's petition was simple and straightforward; she asked only for her own life and the lives of her people. She explained to Ahasuerus that she and her countrymen had been marked out for destruction, and this was the reason she felt compelled to come to him (7:3–4). Were it only a matter of their enslavement, she would have remained silent, but since her people faced total annihilation, her conscience wouldn't allow her to stand by and say nothing.

The king responded by asking who would presume to do such an outrageous thing, which shows that he had no idea his genocidal decree pertained to his queen. Ahasuerus's response, then, implies one of two things: either he didn't know Esther was a Jew (suggested by 3:10–13; note also 2:10, 20) or Haman hadn't told him that the Jews were the object of his decree (suggested by 3:8–9). This question will be addressed shortly, but what matters here is that Esther identified Haman as the culprit; he was the enemy who had plotted to have her and her people completely destroyed. Shocked and enraged, the king immediately dismissed himself from the banquet and went into the palace garden to gather his composure and consider his course of action. Seeing the king's reaction—and now realizing that the queen was herself a Jew—Haman became terrified. His wife and advisors had warned him just hours earlier that he was going to fall before Mordecai because he was a Jew; if Queen Esther was also a Jew, surely his fate was sealed.

This scene represents the turning point in the story with respect to the Jews' future, just as Ahasuerus's sleepless night was the turning point for Mordecai. At the moment Esther voiced her petition, Haman realized that she was Jewish, and he must have sensed that he was in desperate trouble. As he had begun to fall before Mordecai, it now seemed certain that his end was at hand because of the Jews. *How quickly things had changed*—the man, who only a day before had stood triumphant over the Jews, was now on the verge of being destroyed because of them. The writer highlighted this startling reversal, first by giving a glimpse into Haman's mind and then by noting his response. Esther's petition—more precisely, Ahasuerus's reaction to it—terrified Haman because he realized that the king's disposition toward him was turning; he knew his position and power were slipping away. And so when Ahasuerus withdrew to the palace garden, Haman remained behind to beg Esther for his life. Only moments earlier, Esther had been pleading for her life to be delivered from Haman's hands; now he was begging her to intervene on behalf of his.

The psychology of Haman's thinking and response is transparent in the story, but not so with Ahasuerus. The reader must "read between the lines" to discover the reason for his intense reaction to Esther's words. It seems clear he hadn't realized that his decree implicated his beloved wife. Indeed, Haman himself hadn't realized it until that very moment. Now, Ahasuerus was left with an agonizing predicament—he had unwittingly signed Esther's death warrant and was powerless to revoke it. He understood that even he was subject to the edict that bore his seal; it seemed the lot had indeed been cast.

Surely this was part of the reason for the king's outrage, but the larger story suggests that there was more to it. Again, the text doesn't anywhere state that Ahasuerus knew the Jews were the target of his decree. Verse 3:13 allows for that possibility, but three considerations argue otherwise. First, the confidence the king placed in Haman suggests that he'd approve Haman's request without knowing who these people were that refused to honor his laws (ref. again 3:8). Ahasuerus ruled a vast empire comprised of many conquered nations and peoples, none of whom were willing subjects. This wouldn't have been his first experience with rebellion and the ethnicity of the rebels wasn't of concern; all that mattered was crushing any resistance and restoring order to his kingdom. Moreover, the narrative indicates that Ahasuerus's scribes penned the decree as directed by Haman. It carried the king's name and seal, but Haman's content (3:12). Finally, and most importantly, Ahasuerus knew that Mordecai was a Jew and still insisted upon honoring him before his subjects (6:10). He'd have never done this if he knew the Jews were the target of the decree he personally authorized and published throughout his kingdom (3:10–15); that would have been politically disastrous.

Another thing to note is that the text nowhere reveals when or how Esther disclosed her Jewish identity to the king (though most assume she did so at the banquet). The writer only mentions that she told him that day of her relationship with Mordecai (8:1). When the various pieces of data are assembled, a likely scenario emerges: assuming that Ahasuerus was unaware of the specific people group targeted by his decree, Esther would have explained when she made her plea that it pertained to her Jewish countrymen. But in doing so, she also revealed her own Jewish identity (7:3). And learning that the Jews were the object of his edict, Ahasuerus's thoughts would have immediately turned to Mordecai, the Jew whom he'd personally honored only a few hours earlier. He'd just exalted a Jew in the sight of his subjects, and now he was faced with having to own the slaughter of all of the Jews throughout his empire. And if Mordecai did indeed come to the king's mind, it's likely he mentioned him to Esther. For she was the one who brought Ahasuerus the news of the plot against him, but she'd done so in Mordecai's name (ref. 2:22). And if that mention occurred, surely Esther would have told the king that Mordecai was her cousin and the man who'd raised her (note again 8:1).

In the end, no one really knows how the scenario played out, for the writer simply doesn't say. His approach here, as throughout the story, was to omit details that don't contribute to (or might even distract from) the points he wished to emphasize. In this section, he wanted his readers to focus on the fact of Haman's downfall and Mordecai's exaltation, *particularly as this outcome resulted from the convergence of separate providential streams.*

A series of astonishing and unforeseen circumstances had brought Haman to this place, and his fate was now to be sealed by one more irony of providence. When the enraged king retreated to his garden, Haman remained behind to plead with Esther to intervene on his behalf. Terrified and panicked, he groveled before her, eventually throwing himself on the couch where she sat at the very moment Ahasuerus returned to them. Haman was abasing himself before Esther, but it appeared to the king that he was attacking her (7:8). He perhaps thought Haman was about to kill her for exposing him, but the language and context suggest that Ahasuerus believed he was attempting to rape her. The Hebrew verb points in this direction, as does the writer's comment that the king saw Haman "falling on the couch" where Esther was seated. Ahasuerus's reaction also supports this interpretation; he was astonished that Haman would be so bold as to assault his queen while he was present in the palace.

Haman's Demise (7:9–10)

When Ahasuerus saw Haman throwing himself at Esther, he cried out against him. At the king's word, his servants seized Haman and covered his face, symbolizing the sentence of death. So the response of one of the king's eunuchs, "Behold indeed, the gallows standing at Haman's house fifty cubits high…" Ahasuerus misinterpreted Haman's actions, and yet his sentence was perfectly appropriate. Haman was, in part, executed for a crime he didn't commit, but his hanging on the gallows he had built for Mordecai—a man who "spoke good on behalf of the king"—pointedly testified that justice was served. Ahasuerus certainly believed he received what his treachery deserved, for his outrage passed as soon as Haman's body hung lifeless on the gallows.

Mordecai's Exaltation (8:1–2)

Haman's death represented the climactic irony in the story of his relationship with Mordecai. Framed by Mordecai's prophetic declaration in 4:14, the writer carefully traced out Haman's descent from exalted lord and destroyer of the Jewish people to humiliated criminal executed on a Jewish gallows. And yet, his end had only secondary importance. Again, the issue in the unfolding story is not Haman's death as such, but his fall *before Mordecai*; Haman's demise was bound up in Mordecai's triumph. The hand of providence had determined a reversal of fortunes, but one extending beyond the fate of the gallows. It was to be a complete reversal in which the two men effectively traded places. The parade through Susa was simply a foretaste of the remarkable outcome that lay just ahead.

The previous context (6:1–14) predicted that Haman's downfall would be accompanied by Mordecai's ascension, but the current one shows that this reversal amounted to an exchange—*in the process of their individual transformation, each man assumed the other's status and role.* Haman was "lifted up" by meeting death on the gallows he intended for Mordecai, while Mordecai was exalted by gaining everything that had belonged to Haman.

The first thing transferred to Mordecai was Haman's *status* and *position*. Haman had enjoyed a place of preeminence under Ahasuerus, displaying the king's signet ring on his finger. Such rings bore a king's personal seal, and this seal was stamped in wax on the face of official documents to establish their royal origin and binding authority. Thus, a signet ring represents the ruler whose seal it bears; whoever possesses it possesses the authority and power to act in the king's name and on his behalf. Haman held Ahasuerus's signet ring since the day of the decree, but now it was on Mordecai's finger (cf. 3:10, 8:2). He'd taken Haman's place as second only to the king himself.

But the reversal of fortune didn't end there; Mordecai acquired Haman's *house* as well as his position. The king gave his signet ring to Mordecai, but he transferred Haman's house to Esther (8:1a). Here, the word, "house," doesn't refer merely to a physical dwelling, but to everything connected with it. Haman's house encompassed his *household*, which included his servants and attendants as well as his physical property. When Esther set Mordecai over Haman's house (8:2b), she was giving him authority over his entire household. Mordecai had replaced Haman as lord over his house.

Thus, Mordecai fully assumed Haman's place. He supplanted him *politically* as chief ruler over the king's empire and *personally* as head over his house, making his triumph absolute. But the writer didn't end his story here; he recognized that the Mordecai/Haman subplot set the stage for what lay ahead for all of the Jews in Ahasuerus's kingdom. But, even more, it prefigured that outcome; Mordecai's triumph signaled a greater one still to come.

Mordecai's exaltation was a kind of "first fruits" that looked to the full harvest yet to come. His personal triumph anticipated the same outcome for all of his countrymen and also strengthened the expectation that it would indeed occur. So the writer's concern was ultimately not the person of Mordecai (or Esther, for that matter), but the larger, more important matter that the Mordecai subplot prefigured. With Mordecai's triumph complete, he could now turn his attention to the fate of the Hebrew people under the dark shadow of Ahasuerus's invincible decree.

Chapter 6
The Turning of the Lot—the Jews and Their Enemies

An amazing set of circumstances had completely turned the tables on Haman and Mordecai. Haman died the degrading public death he'd planned for Mordecai and Mordecai obtained Haman's distinction as the king transferred to him everything he'd previously granted to Haman. So Esther shared Mordecai's triumph and a new standing with her royal husband; no longer simply his beloved wife, Ahasuerus now knew Esther as the close relative of the man who'd saved his life. *Most importantly, this Persian king had gained a new perspective on the Jews under his reign.* Whatever he'd thought of them before, his experience with Mordecai surely raised his opinion, and all the more when he discovered that the wife he adored and respected was Mordecai's Jewish cousin. But this discovery left Ahasuerus agonized; he now realized that the edict he'd published across his kingdom—the edict he could not repeal—called for the slaughter of all Jews, including his queen and the man he'd rewarded as a loyal subject. Haman was dead, but the decree he'd orchestrated lived on. Unlike its author, the decree was immortal, impervious to every circumstance and human power.

The Counter-Decree (8:3–15)

Realizing that the lot was still cast against her people, Esther again approached Ahasuerus on their behalf. She begged him to revoke Haman's decree, and he responded by affirming his favor toward the Jews; didn't his own actions prove that (8:3–7)? He had no desire to see them killed (how much less Esther and Mordecai), but even he had no power over the decree. He had done what he could as the supreme human authority, but the "law of the Medes and Persians" had absolute authority, even over him; in the Persian empire, law was king. This was precisely the reason Haman had insisted upon this procedure (cf. 1:19, 3:8–14). As desperately as he wanted to, Ahasuerus was unable to grant Esther's request. He could put an end to Haman's life, but not his genocidal designs.

The king was powerless over Haman's decree, but there was something he *could* do—he could issue a *counter-decree* opposing the previous one. In this way, perhaps, he could prevent the slaughter Haman intended. So Ahasuerus instructed Esther to have such a decree written as she saw fit and affix his name and seal to it. In that way, it would carry the same authority and irrevocable status as the one Haman had issued (8:8).

Esther assigned the task to Mordecai who then assembled the king's scribes to compose a new decree per his instruction. And when it was done, Mordecai applied the king's seal—the seal of the signet ring that now adorned his finger. What stands out here is that the writer used the same language as before, intentionally linking the two edicts together (cf. 8:9–10 and 3:12–13). He highlighted them as both addressing the same issue, but with the second one providing the corrective to the first. Haman's decree imposed a day of slaughter that couldn't be averted; Mordecai's authorized and outlined a counter response (8:11–12).

Both edicts were written, authorized, and distributed in exactly the same way; what distinguished them was their authors and their adversarial intent. Each wrote against the other with equal authority, leaving the reader to wonder whose decree would triumph. But the circumstance to this point already suggested the answer. In every possible way—in favor, honor, status, authority, and possessions—Mordecai had supplanted Haman; would it now be different with his decree?

And yet, the one thing that gave the nod to Haman's decree was the fact that it authorized *military* might against the Jews. Not just local civilians, but Ahasuerus's well-armed forces were going to execute their king's decree against the Jews and the added incentive of plunder ensured that these battle-hardened men would undertake their task enthusiastically. Whatever weaponry and strategy the Jews might employ, they'd never be able to prevail against the military power of the indomitable Medo-Persian Empire. Mordecai's decree afforded his countrymen the exact same rights Haman's granted to their enemies (cf. 3:13, 8:13), but rights and the ability to execute them aren't the same thing.

The Response to Mordecai's Decree (8:16–17)

Both edicts were issued first in the capital city of Susa, but the response to them was very different. Haman's had provoked confusion and anxiety (3:15), while Mordecai's brought rejoicing and celebration. In particular, the writer connected the city's jubilation with Mordecai's personal exaltation (8:4–15). Haman, too, had been publicly honored, but the writer conspicuously omitted any mention of the people celebrating him. They paid homage to Haman, but only outwardly because the king commanded it (3:2). On the other hand, the people of Susa wildly celebrated Mordecai; for the Jews especially, his exaltation brought a sense of "light and gladness and joy and honor" (8:16).

The Jews' rejoicing was not at all surprising, but the writer noted that the whole city of Susa shared their joy. Jew and Gentile alike celebrated and that pattern was to be repeated throughout the kingdom. Everywhere the news of the new edict arrived, the Jewish people rejoiced and held festal celebrations, glad for the king's provision for them. And their joy and exultation were infectious as their Gentile neighbors marveled with them at such an amazing turn of events. So also the honor Mordecai enjoyed with the people of Susa came to his fellow Jews; indeed, his decree led many Gentiles to pay them the greatest possible tribute by becoming proselytes to Judaism (8:17). The writer attributed this to "fear of the Jews," but the issue was really fear of the Jews' *God*. The Jews themselves had done nothing to inspire fear and awe; what moved these Gentiles was Ahasuerus's counter-decree, for they perceived in it the astonishing intervention of the Hebrew God.

Mordecai had previously hinted at this powerful hand—the hand of Israel's covenant-keeping Lord—when he told Esther that deliverance would come from somewhere else if she failed to act on behalf of her people (4:14). Then, not many days later, as they observed circumstances beginning to turn against him, Haman's wife and friends warned him that the lot was now clearly on the side of the Jews. They saw in his humiliation at Mordecai's hand a fearful omen of what was to come (6:13). Within hours, their prediction bore fruit as Haman was hanged on the gallows he'd built for Mordecai, and Mordecai assumed Haman's place over his household and in the royal court.

Now, as Mordecai's decree made its way across the vast kingdom, multitudes were beginning to sense what Haman's wife and counselors had—*there was indeed some mysterious power championing these peculiar Israelite people.* Yes, their nation had fallen to foreign powers, and they were reduced to a scattered remnant of defeated exiles, but somehow, this didn't seem to be the last word for them. Ahasuerus's counter-decree certainly reinforced this impression. For what, other than the intervention of a favorable divine power, could possibly explain the radical change of heart of Medo-Persia's sovereign? To many of Ahasuerus's subjects, it seemed clear that the Jews worshipped a powerful and caring deity and such a god was worth knowing and serving. If that meant becoming a Jew, so be it. Not everyone shared this conviction, but to all who took notice of this strange new development, Gentile and Jew alike, it appeared that the light of hope was dawning in a new day after the dark night of Haman's decree; the lot indeed seemed to be turning in the Jews' favor.

Once again, the author implied God's presence and activity but refused to mention him. Of all the places in the story to introduce Israel's God—the One who is the Creator and sovereign Lord of all men—this is the perfect one. In fact, it seems almost impossible that the writer could avoid speaking of him here. He strongly *suggests* God and even glorifies him indirectly by his account of the amazing turn of events, yet he refrains from mentioning him. There's no way this silence could have been accidental; this passage virtually shouts God's name. By not mentioning God in a context where he clearly implicates him, the author leaves no doubt about his intent—*writing to Jewish exiles, he wanted to remind them and underscore that the God who seemed to have abandoned his promise and his people had done neither; his hand wasn't exposed, but it was at work.* Though David's kingdom lay in ruins and the house of Israel was scattered under Gentile rule, the God of Abraham, Isaac, and Jacob remained faithful and committed to the oath he swore to the patriarchs and their descendants. Yes, this tragic circumstance was the result of Israel's unbelief and rebellion, just as Moses and the prophets had warned for centuries. At the same time, they tempered their warning with the assurance that Israel's God would remain faithful to his covenant—not because his people were deserving, but because he'd determined to use Abraham and his offspring to vanquish the curse and restore his creation to himself.

God's steadfast faithfulness was the backstory hinting that Mordecai's triumph, as astonishing as it was, was only a foretaste of what was to come. Looking ahead to the fateful day marked out by the two decrees, the writer held out the hope that deliverance lay in store for all the Jews. Nevertheless, he gave no indication that this hope was anything but thin and unlikely. Queen Esther had done all she could to intervene for her people, but the decree against them stood fast. Even the supreme power and goodwill of the king himself could not deliver them from its power and the slaughter it promised. The only possible remedy was to allow the Jews to defend themselves when the day arrived. But even that, considered realistically, meant little. It was all well and good to grant the Jews the right to fight back against their adversaries, but what chance did a disorganized and ill-equipped band of exiles have against well-trained and well-armed militias?

In the end, every indication was that the counter-decree would have little effect on the outcome; Haman, it seemed, was going to triumph even in death. But in reality, there was another power at work beyond natural circumstances and natural provision. That power, unseen and unnamed, had amazingly turned the king's heart toward the Jews, and the same phenomenon was repeated in the hearts of

Gentiles throughout the kingdom. People who knew nothing of the Jews' God sensed divine favor and power acting on their behalf. To many of them, this intervention was so obvious and compelling that they chose to make this foreign deity their own and joined themselves to his people.

The Jews' Triumph (9:1–16)

Mordecai's personal triumph signaled that the lot was beginning to turn for his countrymen. Thus, the writer immediately shifted his gaze from Mordecai's exaltation to the circumstance of the Jews' deliverance. The balance of the story (apart from the epilogue of chapter 10) records the process of their triumph, which the writer presented in two distinct parts. The first addresses the Jews' victory over their enemies (9:1–16) and the second the outcome of it (9:17–32).

The Jewish and Gentile reaction to Mordecai's decree (8:15–17) forms the prelude to this section and makes a couple of important contributions to it. First, it heightens the reader's sense of anticipation of how things were going to turn out for the Jews. But it also lays the necessary foundation for that outcome. In particular, the change of heart that occurred among the Gentiles would prove to be instrumental in the Jews' remarkable triumph.

The writer began this section with a general statement summarizing the circumstances and outcome of the appointed day (9:1). But he crafted it in a way that hints at supernatural intervention. He noted the Jews' victory over their enemies, but attributed their triumph to forces operating behind the scenes: On the day when their adversaries "hoped to gain the mastery over them, *it was turned to the contrary* so that the Jews themselves gained the mastery over those who hated them."

The mysterious working of providence is a key theme in the book of Esther, but this is one of the few clear allusions to it. Providence works off stage, out of sight and out of mind, and this is the way the writer chose to interact with it. He tells his story so as to make providence a central actor, but an actor that carries out its role behind the scenes. Providence is an imperceptible power, but an effectual one, and this ensures that things are never exactly what they seem to be. The result is that no one is able to judge the meaning, value or import of any particular event or circumstance. Such judgments can be made only in retrospect, and even then only the light of eternity will fully reveal things as they truly are.

So it is with the events in the Esther story. As the storyline unfolds, the permanence of Haman's decree appears as a tragic and terrible providential circumstance. So also the issuing of a counter-decree does little in itself to alter that sense. Though it carried the same royal authority as its predecessor, the wider circumstances leave the unshakeable impression that the Jews' situation remained perilous, if not altogether hopeless. But this is precisely the point; the fact of a *naturally* hopeless predicament allowed for—indeed, it necessitated—a *supernatural* deliverance and triumph.

Anyone looking at the situation would naturally conclude that it would be best if the king were able to revoke Haman's decree and so avoid the day of slaughter altogether. The fact that he could only issue a counter-decree seems to be just one more unfortunate and unhelpful providence. But what men can't discern in the moment God understands. In this circumstance, revoking the initial decree would actually undermine his good purpose—not just for the Jews, but the Gentiles as well. For Haman's decree *created* the Jews' adversaries, so that its demise would mean their demise. And no adversaries meant no deliverance or triumphal victory. Revoking the decree would have solved the problem, but then that human act, rather than divine intervention, would have been the Jews' deliverer.

If Haman's decree were annulled—as both Esther and Mordecai hoped—they and their fellow Israelites would have been robbed of the priceless privilege of witnessing their God come to their rescue. It is precisely the fact of the lot being determined against them that enabled the Jews to experience the triumph of an unimaginable victory over their enemies. Despite how it appeared, the irrevocability of the decree against them was the greatest gift from their God—*by it, he allowed them to share in their forefathers' privilege.* Whether in Egypt (Exod. 7–12), at the Red Sea (Exod. 14), outside the walls of Jericho (Josh. 6), under Gideon's leadership (Judg. 7) or during the Assyrian advance on Jerusalem (Isa. 36–37), their forefathers had witnessed the invincibility of their God's covenant faithfulness. Over and over again, the children of Israel found themselves in seemingly hopeless circumstances, only to have God arise to deliver them with a mighty hand. And this was by design, that they would learn to trust their covenant Lord and Father who'd pledged them to himself, and not their own resources or ingenuity. In each instance, he stripped them of natural remedies—indeed, he stacked the deck against them, so that they'd have no choice but to attribute their triumph to him. And now the Israelite exiles in Persia were about to experience the same sort of intervention.

On the appointed day when the two edicts collided, the Jews throughout the empire rallied together within their communities and prepared themselves as best they could for the assault they knew was coming. But the lot that had turned for Mordecai also embraced his countrymen, so that those who hoped to prevail over the Jews found themselves vanquished by them. The adversaries' design was "turned to the contrary," not so much by a reversal of military fortunes as by a change of heart. The Jews gained mastery over their enemies *because dread had fallen upon them* (cf. 8:17 with 9:1–3).

The text indicates that this Gentile dread had both a passive and active effect; many refused to rise up against the Jews while others actively came to their defense. Among those defenders were the king's provincial rulers, who likely provided the Jews with weapons and supplies in addition to using their authority to discourage attacks. These rulers, too, acted out of dread, but specifically dread of *Mordecai*, and that because of the reputation he had gained among them. Here again, the writer implies that providence played a crucial role. Ahasuerus promoted Mordecai at the time of Haman's death, but it would have taken some time for his reputation to grow and his fame to spread throughout such a sprawling empire (9:4). Without that time—in this case, nine months (ref. again 8:7–14), Mordecai wouldn't have gained the widespread recognition and respect among the king's rulers that motivated them to come to the aid of his people. So also those months allowed sufficient time for the considerable logistical task of arming and provisioning the Jews scattered across the empire.

In spite of all these favorable providences, some groups did rise up against the Jews, but their attacks were unsuccessful. The Jews "struck all their enemies with the sword, killing and destroying" (9:5). The author chose this description to highlight the absolute reversal of fate—the turning of the lot. The Jews killed and destroyed those whom Haman's decree authorized to kill and destroy them (cf. 3:13). They triumphed with the edge of the sword, but this victory was more than the natural outcome of good preparation and fierce fighting. The writer makes this clear by emphasizing the *one-sidedness* of the conflict—the Jews were able to do whatever they pleased to their enemies.

In every village, town, and community across the empire, wherever men took up arms against them, the Jews prevailed over their adversaries in great victories reminiscent of the triumphal battle of Jericho. And though the writer didn't state that no Jewish lives were lost in the fighting, his silence regarding that issue certainly leaves that impression, especially when he was so careful to document the Gentile deaths (9:6–16). At the very least, he wanted his readers to understand the complete lopsidedness of the Israelite victory. At the end of the two days of fighting, more than seventy-five thousand lay dead and the enemies of the Jews were no more.

From his general discussion of the conflict, the writer narrowed his focus to the capital city of Susa. The fighting there resulted in the Jews killing five hundred men along with Haman's ten sons (9:6–10). The account is brief but filled with important insight. First, it highlights the restraint exercised by the Jews. Mordecai's edict, paralleling Haman's, authorized his countrymen to slay women and children. But whereas Haman's edict called for the slaughter of Jewish women and children with the goal of annihilating all of the Jews in the empire, Mordecai's made no such demand. It simply *allowed* for the killing of women and children as necessary in the cause of self-defense (ref. 8:11). And so it's significant that the writer doesn't mention women or children being killed by the Jews (9:6). This suggests that the attackers were primarily (if not entirely) men. But more importantly, it points to the Jewish response being purely defensive and not in any way hateful or vindictive. Unlike their Gentile adversaries, they had no interest in taking innocent lives.

As well, the Jews in Susa didn't take any plunder from those they defeated, though Mordecai's decree granted this also as a reciprocal right (cf. 8:11 with 3:13). And as it was in Susa, so it was throughout the provinces (ref. 9:15–16). The fact that the writer mentioned this behavior three times (ref. 9:10, 15–16) shows that he believed it to be important to his story, although he doesn't say *why* he believed this. Neither did he explain the reason the Jews refused to take spoil from those they killed. He evidently believed his Israelite audience would understand and so felt no need to explain. But other readers don't share this insight and so must consider the likely explanations.

One possibility is that religious concerns motivated the refusal to take spoil. That is, the Jews viewed the property of their Gentile enemies as *unclean*. But if this were the case, why would Mordecai authorize it in the first place? He shared the religious convictions of his countrymen and wouldn't have directed them to do something that defiled them. Another explanation has to do with ethical considerations. It's clear that the Jews viewed their actions as self-defense rather than warfare. And this being the case, it's possible they saw no justification for taking their adversaries' property as plunder. But perhaps the best answer for the Jews' refusal—one that well explains the writer's emphasis on it—is that they recognized their victory as coming from elsewhere, and the spoils belong to the true victor. *They didn't plunder their enemies because the spoils weren't rightfully theirs.* If this view is correct, this circumstance makes its own contribution to the story's core theme of God's providential faithfulness—that is, his unwavering commitment to fulfill his purposes and promises.

Whatever the actual reasons for this behavior, it presents a sharp contrast between the Jews and their adversaries. The promise of plunder has always been an incentive to take up arms. Few will risk their lives for nothing other than someone else's glory, power, and profit. Hatred is a motive that is oftentimes sufficient to provoke the killing of innocents, whether or not it occurs in war. But hatred becomes all the more compelling when combined with the prospect of personal material gain. (This dynamic was powerfully displayed in the Nazi treatment of Jews during Hitler's rule.) But the Jews here had no such motivation; they neither hated those who came against them nor desired their property. They sought only to defend themselves and their families. They had a legal right to plunder their attackers, but no interest in doing so.

The writer's account of this conflict also highlights the outcome for Haman's sons. Two things in particular stand out. The first is the *way* he recounted their deaths. Of the thousands who were slain, he identified only these ten men by name. Clearly the writer had more in mind than simply identifying Haman's sons as among those who fought against the Jews and died. By naming them and noting their relation to their father, he was again reinforcing how completely the lot had turned (6:13). Haman's ten sons were an important part of his personal preeminence (5:11), so that their death—which paralleled his own—underscored the fulfillment of the prediction of his complete downfall. The second thing that stands out is the *apparent contradiction* in the account of their deaths. The text first indicates that Haman's sons were slain in Susa along with five hundred other men on the thirteenth day of the month (9:6–11). But then the writer has Esther petitioning the king to have Haman's sons hanged on a gallows the next day (9:12–14). But a closer look shows that there's no contradiction; Esther wasn't asking that Haman's sons be executed by hanging as their father had been, but that their *dead bodies* be put on public display in Susa by hanging them on poles. This was a common practice in ancient Middle Eastern cultures, and its purpose was to shame the dead person and/or publicly portray him as a criminal or evildoer (ref. Deut. 21:22; 1 Sam. 31:8–13; Ezra 6:11).

In addition to requesting that the bodies of Haman's sons be hanged on poles, Esther also asked Ahasuerus to allow the fighting to continue for a second day (9:13a). Some commentators have struggled with this petition, finding it out of character for Esther. Asking to extend the time of slaughter seems to show a vengeful spirit, especially in light of her request concerning Haman's dead sons. These things might offend modern sensibilities, but Esther was motivated by concern for her countrymen and an end to the fighting, not malice or vengeance. The context suggests that she knew enemies remained in Susa and she wanted the Jews there to be able to defend themselves after the appointed day had passed (9:15–16). So publicly displaying the bodies of Haman's sons might minimize further bloodshed by discouraging those who were not yet ready to give up the fight.

The Festival of Purim (9:17–32)

The Jews' remarkable deliverance is the climax of the story and the goal the writer had in mind when he penned his account. Again, he detailed it in two distinct parts (9:1–16 and 9:17–32). He transitioned into this section by summarizing the Jewish and Gentile response to Mordecai's decree (8:15–17) and then described the actual conflict with its triumphal outcome. Finally, he concluded the story by relating how the Jews established the annual festival of Purim to commemorate their great victory.

God's covenant people escaped what appeared to be certain destruction, but with an overwhelming and absolute triumph. Those who sought to eradicate the Jews found themselves completely eradicated over the span of only two days. It was no wonder the Jewish reaction across the empire was exultation and great celebration. The Jews outside of Susa celebrated on the fourteenth of Adar while their brethren in Susa continued the fight a second day. Those Jews then observed their own day of feasting and celebration on the fifteenth of the month (9:17–19).

But such a monumental victory—one akin to the great deliverances of the past—deserved more than those two days of celebration; it warranted perpetual, formal recognition in an annual commemoration. And so it was that Mordecai immediately set about establishing the festival of *Purim* as a national holiday to be celebrated every year from that time forward (9:20–28).

Months earlier, Mordecai had written to his Jewish brethren throughout the empire authorizing them to resist their enemies on the day of slaughter. Now, he was writing again, first to set down a permanent record of the events of their great national victory, but also to pen a new edict for his countrymen. Henceforth, they were to set apart the fourteenth and fifteenth of Adar—the days when they'd rested in triumph over their enemies—as an annual celebration. And as they had triumphed in solidarity as Abraham's covenant children, so they were to celebrate in the same way. Purim was not to be a private, personal holiday, but a *community* festival marked by mutual concern and care. Every Jew was to participate in the celebration and feasting, and this meant exchanging food gifts with one another, especially being careful to provide such gifts to the poor among them. No one was to be left out of the festivities. For months, the Jews had dreaded Adar as a time that would see destruction and mourning, but instead it brought deliverance and triumph beyond anyone's wildest dream. Therefore, this entire month was to be a month of great joy and delight—a month having its focus in the appointed festivities of the fourteenth and fifteenth days (9:22).

When the Jews received Mordecai's letters, they "undertook what they had started to do" (9:23). Across the vast kingdom, Jewish communities had celebrated their own local victory over their attackers, and they rejoiced to learn of Mordecai's plan to establish an annual, national celebration. What each community had done independently, they would now do every year in solidarity. However isolated they were from one another, the Jews' shared triumph over a shared enemy bound them together in a new way. Haman had "cast Pur" against them collectively and without distinction, and they'd together enjoyed the turning of the lot. He'd done so believing the Pur secured the future and the future was his (ref. again 3:7–13). But other forces were at work, and the providential interweaving of numerous independent circumstances and events fashioned a different outcome—indeed, an outcome antithetical to what Haman expected. His wicked scheme "which he had devised against the Jews" was "returned on his own head" (9:25).

Haman had foolishly placed his confidence in the predictive insight of the lot (*pur*), unable to see that his—and every human—lot is subject to another power, which casts its own *pur*. Haman's lot was powerless over the future, and for this reason, its insight was useless. If it couldn't secure the future, it couldn't actually predict it. Whatever his confidence in it, Haman's lot was a false lot that turned against him; the true lot—the triumphant lot—was in the hand of another, and thus the festival commemorating the Jews' triumph was aptly named *Purim*—"lots" (9:26–32).

Haman had "cast Pur" regarding the Jews, but so had their God and his lot trumped Haman's. Yahweh cast his lot on behalf of Israel when he made his covenant with Abraham, and the Israelites had since witnessed the lot's favor many times. They experienced it in Egypt and at the Red Sea and throughout their centuries in Canaan. Again and again, the children of Israel cried out to their covenant Father in their need, and he rescued them. Esther's generation of exiles knew that history and clung to the same hope (ref. 4:1–3). And now they'd learned for themselves what their forefathers experienced; no earthly lot would prevail against the lot cast by the God of Abraham, Isaac and Jacob.

The *pur* of God's covenant oath and faithfulness set aside the one cast for the Jews' destruction, and it was fitting that such a glorious triumph should be memorialized by all Israel and their allies in every place throughout their generations. The Glory of Israel had demonstrated once more that he is not a man that he should lie or change his mind; his lovingkindness (covenant integrity) is everlasting, and his faithfulness endures to all generations. Mordecai— and the Jews in solidarity with him—instituted Purim, not to commemorate their own victory as such, but to celebrate their covenant God and Father who remains ever faithful to the oath he swore to Abraham. Whatever befell them, he would remain Israel's God for the sake of his purposes.

Mordecai initially sent out letters to all the provinces calling for an annual celebration on the fourteenth and fifteenth of Adar (9:20–21), and he and Esther followed this up with a formal edict specifying how the feast of Purim was to be celebrated (9:30–31). The writer described this document as "words of peace and truth," which points to its significance rather than its instruction. The edict prescribed the particulars of the Purim commemoration, but the festival itself spoke of and celebrated *peace* and *truth*. It was an annual reminder, not of the "peace" that is victory over enemies, but the *shalom* that is wholeness, well-being, and flourishing associated with God's favor and blessing. And Purim speaks of sha-lom because it celebrates the God of truth who always upholds his good and wise designs and keeps his promises. Esther's "command" (9:32) spoke of peace and truth in that it called the Jews to for-ever commemorate their privilege and blessing as God's covenant people, and so celebrate the God who is true; the God who never changes and never forgets.

So also the edict established "times of fasting and their lam-entations" in connection with Purim (9:31). At first glance, this seems strange given the festival's triumphal and celebratory nature; what place do fasting and lamentation have in such an occasion? And yet, the edict instructed the Jews that Purim was to be as much about mourning and fasting as feasting and celebration. The reason becomes clear in the light of the festival's background: *The great triumph Purim commemorates was conceived in the womb of woe and desperation.* It had its origin in dark days of threat, helplessness, lamentation, and fasting in which the Jews sought the intervention of their covenant God. By prescribing these practices as part of the Purim festival, Mordecai and Esther were ensuring that their countrymen would never forget the nature, source, and greatness of their deliverance. Israel's ever-faithful God had brought them out of death into life.

Epilogue
Mordecai's Tribute

The Esther story reaches its climax with the Jews' stunning victory over those who sought to destroy them. The writer then closed it out with a brief commentary focusing on Mordecai and his legacy (10:1–3). But why end the story this way? Why focus on Mordecai rather than recapping the Jews' triumph and how it played out for them? The answer seems to be the close connection between Mordecai and his fellow exiles; his ordeal and triumph were theirs. They shared the same humiliation and death sentence and enjoyed the same deliverance and victory over their foes. *The reader, then, is supposed to see in this summary of Mordecai's greatness the greatness of the entire Hebrew nation.* Yes, exile and subjugation to Gentile powers were going to continue for the Jewish people; Mordecai himself continued to be subject to King Ahasuerus. But together, they had prevailed over their enemies such that those enemies were no more. The unseen hand that preserved, delivered, and exalted Mordecai reached out to his fellow exiles in the same way.

This perspective also speaks to the question of why the writer didn't mention Esther in his closing summary. This seems especially strange given her central place in the story and its sequence of events. But Esther, too, shared Mordecai's triumph and legacy of greatness. He was exalted to rule as second only to King Ahasuerus, but she exercised the unique power and influence reserved for the king's beloved and trusted queen. Mordecai had free access to the royal court, but Esther had access to the royal chambers. Ahasuerus respected and honored Mordecai, but his heart belonged to Esther.

She had his devotion, and so his ear, in a way that no man, not even Mordecai, could claim.

Perhaps the most notable feature of the epilogue is the way the writer depicted Mordecai's greatness—he described it in terms of his relationship with the king. And not just any king, *but the ruler who embodied the Gentile power presiding over Israel's suffering in exile and captivity.* Even when he spoke of Mordecai's honored standing among his Jewish brethren, the writer did so in terms of his status as a ruler in the Medo-Persian kingdom. Explaining Mordecai's greatness in terms of Ahasuerus's imperial greatness is, to say the least, a curious way for a Jewish writer to conclude his story about Jewish triumph over Gentile powers. And yet, he hinted at this perspective from the story's beginning. He began his account, not with Mordecai or Esther or even the Jews' plight, but an elaborate description of the majesty and splendor of Ahasuerus's kingdom and reign (1:1–7).

Thus, the writer ended his story the way he began it. But he was doing more than providing a suitable bookend. He was intentionally framing Mordecai's greatness in terms of the greatness of the man he'd introduced and described at the outset, the king who was the supreme Near Eastern ruler at that time. And Ahasuerus was indeed a great man; he ruled an immense kingdom of 127 provinces stretching from India to Ethiopia. Merely establishing such an empire within the limitations of the ancient world is itself an astonishing feat, and only Alexander the Great rivaled it. But Ahasuerus was able to hold his empire together and bring it into submission to his rule. The authority and power of his dominion were such that he was able to exact tribute payments from even the most distant and remote of his provincial holdings.

There's no wonder, then, that Ahasuerus's reign was chronicled in the official Medo-Persian records. Such accounts were common in the ancient world (cf. 1 Kings 11:41, 14:29, 15:7, 23, 31, etc.) and served at least two important purposes. First, they provided an enduring legacy for kings; they ensured that the memory of their reign and accomplishments would continue. But, even more, they facilitated national continuity and unity from generation to generation. They did so by providing a historical narrative that helped a people group define and understand themselves. King Ahasuerus and his reign epitomized the Medo-Persian alliance and rightly belonged in their official chronicles, *but what place did a Jewish exile have in them—a man whose people and nation Ahasuerus ruled?* That Ahasuerus would exalt Mordecai to a position of authority and honor is remarkable; that Mordecai should be immortalized alongside the Persian king he served is beyond astonishing. Such was Mordecai's greatness that even his Gentile overlords recognized and commemorated it.

The writer wanted to pay tribute to Mordecai, and there was no better way to demonstrate and extol his greatness than to note his place alongside the great kings of Media and Persia. And so, what might seem at first glance to denigrate Mordecai actually exalts him. His triumph over Haman culminated, in a very real way, with his triumph over all Medo-Persia; Mordecai the powerless, exiled Jew became second only to King Ahasuerus himself. The writer emphasized Mordecai's regal status, but was also careful to show that his greatness didn't reside in his authority and power as such, but in the way he employed them. Mordecai wielded his power as a *servant-ruler*, not for his own benefit or glory, but the good of his people and nation (10:3). In this way, Mordecai resembled another great figure in Israel's history—*Joseph*, the Hebrew exile in Egypt whose rule as second only to Pharaoh brought life and well-being to his family as well as the Egyptian people.

Like Joseph, Mordecai ruled as the servant of his people, but in a way that honored his Gentile king and his subjects. This is obvious from his inclusion in the Medo-Persian chronicles; only loyal devotion to King Ahasuerus and faithful service on behalf of his kingdom could earn the honor of such a memorial. In this way, too, Mordecai extended his triumph over Haman: Haman pursued greatness, while Mordecai exhibited it; Haman used his position to exalt and profit himself at others' expense, while Mordecai exalted and served his king and his people; Haman memorialized himself in self-serving actions ending in a humiliating public death; Mordecai was granted the lasting memorial of commemoration with the great rulers of Media and Persia. Haman demanded honor, and Mordecai received it, not only from his Jewish countrymen, but the Gentiles whom he ruled in Ahasuerus's name. All—Jew and Gentile alike—recognized and lauded Mordecai's greatness.

Thus, Mordecai prefigured another who was yet to come—another son of Abraham and servant-ruler who would seek the good of his people and speak peace to those under his rule.

> Rejoice greatly, O daughter of Zion, shout for joy, O daughter of Jerusalem! Behold, your king is coming to you; He is just and endowed with salvation [deliverance], humble, and mounted on a donkey, even on a colt, the foal of a donkey. And I will cut off the chariot from Ephraim, and the horse from Jerusalem; and the bow of war will be cut off. And He will proclaim peace to the nations. His dominion shall be from sea to sea, and from the River to the ends of the earth. (Zech. 9:9–10)

The writer's closing commentary focuses on Mordecai's greatness, but so as to spotlight the turn of the lot at the heart of the story. Mordecai's glorious end was the unexpected and seemingly impossible outcome of a death sentence against him and his fellow exiles under Persian rule. The lot had been cast against them, and it seemed that their fate was sealed. More importantly, it appeared that their God had forsaken them. Centuries of unbelief, rebellion, and disobedience had left the Israelite kingdom in ruins and its people in exile under foreign rule. But this circumstance came about, not as an outburst of divine anger, but as the inevitable outcome of God's patient pleading falling on stony hearts. From the days of Moses and throughout their generations, God continually warned the people of Israel that this was coming (ref. Deut. 28:1–69; Josh. 23:1–16). Indeed, his warnings continued right up until the siege of Jerusalem (cf. Jer. 7:19–27, 36:1–3, 37:1–10), yet to no avail. Even afterward, the Lord raised up prophets among the exiles so that they would never forget why this calamity had befallen them (ref. Hag., Zec., and Mal.; cf. also Neh. 9 and Dan. 9:1–19).

So the Israelites who received Haman's death sentence recognized that they deserved their fate and had no right to expect their God to come to their aid. He'd abandoned his sanctuary during their fathers' generation and hadn't returned, though the temple had been rebuilt in Jerusalem. *If he hadn't returned to his holy mountain, why would he come to them in a distant, pagan land?* Yahweh had indeed departed from Israel and gone silent, but he hadn't abandoned his oath to their fathers. His intent for Abraham's offspring remained, so that when the Jews under Ahasuerus's decree cried out to him, he heard their cries and arose on their behalf, just as he had done with their forefathers in Egypt and during the time of the Judges. He laid hold of the lot that had promised their annihilation and turned its prediction back on the head of the one who had cast it. Not Haman's lot, but Yahweh's lot would determine the fate of his people.

In this way, the book of Esther highlights the crucial truth that, in all things under the sun, the story isn't really the story. *What meets the eye in circumstance and experience serves an ultimate design and outcome that are unseen—an outcome that accords with the unchanging purposes bound up in the will and word of the living God.* This means that no one—not even the most mature and faithful Christian— is able to discern the true significance of the situations and events of this life. God's people must look beyond what is seen and guard against judging and responding based on personal experience. Their difficulties, struggles, and suffering are not the story, but neither are their earthly blessings. Christians must look past their circumstances and rest in their Father's stated purpose and ends; it is those realities and his promises regarding them that give meaning to the things that occur in the course of their daily lives.

Nothing is easier than for people—Christians and non-Christians alike—to attach God's promises to *their* desires and expectations and then judge his love and faithfulness based on what happens in their lives and how they view those things. But God is committed to *his* designs, not ours. And even when we have his designs in view, we still cannot judge circumstances and specific outcomes because we lack the ability to see how they contribute to those designs. God works all things *together* for good (Rom. 8:28), which means that the good is in the final outcome, not necessarily the particulars or process. God's promised good is found in the whole that is the fullness of his work in his Son, but human beings can only experience and interact with the parts that pertain to them and are accessible to them.

The same challenge faced the Jewish exiles living under Persian rule. They were obligated to trust their God, the covenant oath he'd made to their fathers, and his faithfulness in keeping it. Haman's decree—an unchangeable decree carrying the king's seal—told them that their destruction was assured, but they followed Mordecai's direction and fasted and prayed to their God who is the great king over all the earth, the God who, centuries earlier, rescued their Hebrew ancestors in a mighty work of redemption because of the oath he'd sworn to Abraham, Isaac, and Jacob (cf. Exod. 3:1–10, 11:1–14:31, 20:1–2). His covenant oath brought their forefathers out of Egypt; perhaps it would deliver them. And indeed, their God did deliver them, not because of their pitiful cries, but because of his own faithfulness. And then not through a spectacular display of supernatural power, but through the invisible and unobtrusive hand of natural providence. The God who seemed absent and disengaged remained committed and faithful. Whatever the circumstances, he would uphold his covenant with Abraham and his offspring, not because of them, but in spite of them. And not ultimately for their sake, but for his sake—for the sake of his glorious, unchanging purpose for the world to be accomplished in the "fullness of the times" in Abraham's promised "seed" (cf. Gen. 12:1–3 with Matt. 1:1; John 8:31–58; Gal. 3).

Thus the story of Esther is a powerful testimony to the God who "keeps covenant," even in his apparent absence and under impossible circumstances. So the story also highlights the obligation of his people to live by faith in their covenant-keeping God. However perilous and hopeless their circumstance, Esther, Mordecai, and their fellow exiles were obliged to trust the word, faithfulness, and power of Israel's God. And so it is with his people today. In every generation, the children of Israel were compelled to trust their God who promised a future day of redemption and renewal; we who are Christians must trust the same God who has now fulfilled his promises in Jesus the Messiah. The Israelite faithful died without having received what was promised; we are those upon whom the ends of the ages have come, so that the faithful of old are now made complete in the Messiah together with us who share in him and his resurrection life (Heb. 11:32–40; cf. Gal. 3:15–4:7).

God's unwavering faithfulness to his eternal intention and promises is the central, unseen thread woven through the Esther story. Its Jewish readers recognized this and later highlighted this theme in a postscript added to the book. This postscript is found in the *Septuagint*, which is the Greek translation of the Old Testament produced by Jewish scholars in the two centuries before Jesus' birth. (There are two distinct versions of this Greek text that survive to this day.) Though not part of the inspired Hebrew text, this addendum contributes to the story by focusing the reader's gaze on key ideas that are critical to its meaning. The postscript picks up where the scriptural account leaves off and it presents its message in characteristic Jewish form as an interpreted dream (cf. Gen. 28:1–17 with 31:1–13, also 37:1–10, 40:1–41:45; Judg. 7:12–15; Dan. 2:1–49, 4:1–37, 7:1–28). The dream came to Mordecai, and he was the one who discerned its meaning.

Here is a rendering of the Septuagint text (drawn from both versions):

> The Jew Mordecai was next in rank to King Ahasuerus, in high standing among the Jews, and was regarded with favor by his many brethren, as the promoter of his people's welfare and the herald of peace for his whole race. Then Mordecai said:
>
> "This is the work of God. For I recall the dream I had about these very things, and not a single detail has been left unfulfilled—the tiny spring that grew into a river, the light of the sun, the abundant waters. The river is Esther, whom the king married and made queen. The two dragons are myself and Haman. The nations are those

who assembled to destroy the name of the Jews. And my people is Israel who cried to God and were saved. Yahweh has saved His people and has rescued us from all these evils.

God worked signs and great wonders, such as have not occurred among the nations. For this purpose He arranged two lots: one for the people of God, the second for all the other nations. These two lots were fulfilled in the hour, the time, and the day of judgment before God and among all the nations. And God remembered His people and rendered justice to His inheritance. And all the people cried out in a loud voice and said, 'Blessed are you, Lord, who remembers the covenants made with our fathers! Amen!' And these days in the month of Adar, on the fourteenth and fifteenth of that same month, will be observed by them with a gathering together with joy and rejoicing before God, from generation to generation forever among His people Israel."

This addendum shows that the Jews who translated the Septuagint understood the significance of the Esther story for the covenant household of Israel. *Most importantly, they interpreted the Esther story in the light of Israel's role in God's larger purposes for the world.* Almost two thousand years earlier, God made a covenant with Abraham to bless all of the earth's families through him and his descendants. The children of Israel were those descendants, and these Jewish translators recognized that God's enduring covenant faithfulness and delivering hand raised on behalf of the Israelite exiles had in view his determination to draw all people to himself through Abraham's "seed," the Israelite in whom Israel would fulfill its covenant vocation (cf. again Gen. 12:1–3 with Isa. 11:1–12, 49:1–6, 53:1–55:5; Amos 9:11–12; Micah 4:1–5; Zech. 2:1–13, 8:1–23).

One day, the exultant joy of the exiles in Medo-Persia—the celebration to be shared by all subsequent generations of Israelites—

would characterize the entire human world. One day, the faithful God of Israel would again arise in remembrance of his covenant and his oath to Abraham to bless all the earth's families through him. In that day, all tribes, tongues, nations, and people would celebrate Purim, not as divine deliverance from human enemies, but as the Creator's hand raised against the invincible powers of sin, death and hell. The pattern of deliverance Israel had enjoyed through the centuries would see its own fulfillment as Yahweh arose to *save*, not with a physical deliverance, but a spiritual one. In that day, deliverance would involve the *forgiveness of sin* by virtue of God's tender mercy— forgiveness bringing the reconciliation and restoration the Jews had longingly awaited since their exile began. This deliverance would usher in the everlasting kingdom hinted at in Eden, embedded in God's covenant oath to Abraham and Israel, and expressly pledged to David.

Purim itself upheld and perpetuated Israel's hope that the God of Abraham, Isaac and Jacob, Moses and David, would prove faithful to fulfill his covenant promises, whatever circumstances might argue against it. Like Passover, Purim spoke of the triumphal deliverance of the Israelite people in spite of their unfaithfulness. But Purim differed from Passover in that it celebrated a deliverance that came in the midst of Israel's exile *and didn't bring it to an end*. Thus, Purim commemorated an episode which itself bolstered the Jews' hope in a *future* deliverance—the ultimate deliverance they longed for, which would end Israel's long night of alienation and exile by addressing their underlying sin and so reconcile them with their covenant Father. This was Israel's *messianic* hope held out by her prophets: In that day of deliverance, the promised son of Abraham and David would bring ultimate liberation and restoration by destroying the true enemies, purging sin and uncleanness, restoring Yahweh's sanctuary, and establishing his everlasting kingdom. And the end of Israel's alienation and exile would mean life for the world as Messiah began rebuilding God's covenant house in himself (cf. Zech. 6:9–15 with John 2:13–21, 12:23–32; Eph. 2:11–22; 1 Peter 2:4–10). In that day, the Lord wouldn't merely be king in Israel, but king over all the earth (Pss. 2, 47, 110; Zech. 9:9–10).

The story of Esther (and the Purim festival) celebrates God's preservation of his people from certain death at the hands of their enemies. But it does so with a conscious sense of his larger purpose in it: The Lord was upholding the Abrahamic household in view of the day when it would give birth to the messianic "seed" he'd promised to Abraham. At the appointed time, and according to his word through his prophets, that offspring would arise in Israel as Abraham's faithful covenant son—the Israelite in whom Israel was predestined to find its true identity and fulfill its calling to bring God's blessing of forgiveness and reconciliation to all the world. And he would minister the Abrahamic blessing as the regal son of David, building the Lord's everlasting sanctuary as his enthroned Priest-King and Prince of Peace (cf. Isa. 9:1–7; Zech. 6:9–15 with Matt. 16:13–18, 28:18–20; John 1:14, 4:19–26; Acts 2:22–39; note also 1 Cor. 3:16–17, 6:12–19).

The Lord pledged the messianic "day" and Israel waited for it with anxious longing. And when at last that day arrived, Jesus of Nazareth came into the world as Israel's deliverer and consolation (cf. Matt. 1:1, 17; Luke 1:26–33, 67–79, 2:25–38). He came to end the exile of Abraham's children and restore them to their God by embodying Israel in himself as Yahweh's faithful Son (cf. Exod. 4:22–23 and Isa. 1:1–8 with Luke 3:21–22, 4:1–13; John 8:28–58). In him, Israel became Israel *indeed* and commenced its mission of global blessing unto the Father's goal of gathering all the earth's families to himself (cf. Isa. 49:1–13 with Matt. 16:13–18, 28:18–20) and finally summing up all things in the creation in his Messiah-Son (Eph. 1:9–10; also 1 Cor. 15:20–28). And we who are found in him are the beneficiaries of that purpose and accomplishment. We, Jew and Gentile alike, enjoy the deliverance for which Israel waited—the deliverance that was in view when God arose on behalf of Mordecai, Esther, and the Jewish exiles scattered throughout Medo-Persia.

And so we, too, celebrate Purim, not as keeping the Jewish festival or as merely looking back to the historical deliverance it commemorates, but as those who stand in the ultimate triumph it anticipated. We celebrate the God of the great and final deliverance, the faithful One of Israel who arose in the fullness of the times to fulfill his ancient oath to Eve, the Patriarchs, the people of Israel, David, and the prophets and ultimately all of Adam's race and the entire creation. We celebrate the One who turned the lot in our favor so that we should not perish at the hand of the destroying powers, but find deliverance, life, and exaltation through the abiding faithfulness, mercy, and power of the Lord who triumphs over all. To him be the glory in the church and in Christ Jesus to all generations forever and ever. So shall it be.

> Blessed be the Lord God of Israel, for He has visited us and accomplished redemption for His people, and has raised up a horn of salvation for us in the house of David His servant—as He spoke by the mouth of His holy prophets from of old—salvation from our enemies, and from the hand of all who hate us; to show mercy toward our fathers, and to remember His holy covenant, the oath which He swore to Abraham our father, to grant us that we, being delivered from the hand of our enemies, might serve Him without fear, in holiness and righteousness before Him all our days. And you, John [the promised forerunner], will be called the prophet of the Most High; for you will go on before the Lord to prepare His ways; to give to His people the knowledge of salvation that is in the forgiveness of their sins, by virtue of the tender mercy of our God, with which the Sunrise from on high shall visit us, to shine upon those who sit in darkness and the shadow of death, to guide our feet into the way of peace. (Luke 1:68–79)

Oh, the depth of the riches both of the wisdom and knowledge of God! How unsearchable are his judgments and unfathomable his ways! For who has known the mind of the Lord, or who became his counselor? Or who has first given to him that it might be paid back to him again? For from him and through him and to him are all things. To him be the glory forever. Amen!

About the Author

Christopher Culver is a graduate of Trinity Bible College and Seminary (MA, MDiv). He has served in pastoral ministry for twenty-five years and has been the pastor of Sovereign Grace Community Church in Denver since its founding in 2002. He and his wife, Denise, make their home in Littleton, Colorado.